Woodworking *for*

Homes for Birds and Mammals

by Carrol L. Henderson
DNR Nongame Wildlife Supervisor

Michael Haake (1958–1990) was an avid conservationist whose life was filled with appreciation for Minnesota's fish and wildlife. He enjoyed fishing and canoeing in the Boundary Waters Canoe Area Wilderness. His yard in Ham Lake, Minn., was his personal nature preserve. It contained an organic garden, four bird feeders, a bat house, and two bird nest boxes.

After Michael's passing in 1990 due to an automobile accident, memorial gifts were donated by Michael's parents to the Nongame Wildlife Fund in the Department of Natural Resources to help fund the production of this book.

Credits

Graphic Design – Colleen Cronin-Anfang, Linda Escher, Adele Smith, *Photography** – Ron Andrews, Dominique Braud, Cornell Lab of Ornithology, H. Cruickshank/VIREO, Ray Cunningham, Carol Dorff, Dr. Bruce Edinger, Dan Engel, C. H. Greenewalt/VIREO, Ed Harp, Katherine Haws, Jeff W. Hedtke, Carrol Henderson*, Ted Johnson, Steve Kittelson, Earl Kopischke, James LaVigne, William H. Longley, John Mathisen, E. S. Morton/VIREO, Dr. Gary Neuchterlein, Dr. Scott Nielsen, Dick Peterson, D. B. Pettingill/VIREO, John Schladweiler, Paul Schmitt, Gregory K. Scott, T. Simmons, Tim Smalley, Carl R. Sams II and J. F. Stoick/VIREO, Theodore Tempest, Fred K. Truslow/ Cornell Lab of Ornithology, Steven Wilson, Wisconsin DNR, J. R. Woodward/VIREO, and Dr. Mike Zicus

* Photos by Carrol Henderson except as noted by photos of other photographers.

Woodworking Plans – Dave Ahlgren, Janice Orr Hage, Carrol L. Henderson, Paul Hedlund, Mary Miller and Judy Voigt-Englund

Text Editors – Jan Ahlgren, Pam Perry, and Catherine Mix

Copy Preparation – Janice Orr Hage

Disclaimer

The use of trade names or references to specific companies or products in this publication does not imply endorsement by the Department of Natural Resources. They are included only as an aid to the reader.

Minnesota DNR
500 Lafayette Road
St. Paul, MN 55155-4040

612-296-6157 (Metro Area)
1-800-766-6000 (MN Toll-free)

Printed on Recycled Paper

TDD (Telecommunications Device for Deaf)
612-296-5484 (Metro Area)
1-800-657-3929 (MN Toll-free)

:ontents

:e wood duck.

Part 3 59

Nest boxes and platforms for use in lakes, rivers, marshes, ponds, and adjacent upland habitats

Part 4 79

Woodworking Plans to Help You Build Your Own Birdhouses. Figures 1 through 27

Thanks 111

The DNR appreciates the involvement of dedicated biologists, artists, photographers, and carpenters who have each contributed their expertise.

A house wren pauses before entering its nest box.

Intro

One of my fond childhood memories is that of being invited by my grandfather—Martin Holland—to visit the woodshop in his basement. He had a wonderful knack for building wooden toys for us grandchildren—toy barns, houses, garages, and wagons. But one time he was making something different—a wren house. It was like magic watching the small pieces of wood being transformed into a little house. Painting was the last step. I helped add the blue and white paint to the house.

Once dry, there was great anticipation as we hung the wren house under the eave of the garage on our farm near Zearing, Iowa.

Again, like magic, the wrens showed up shortly thereafter. They began filling the nest box with twigs. Their beautiful bubbling song was a highlight in our yard that spring, and for many years thereafter. As the wrens hatched their eggs and fed their young, they were a constant source of fascination for our impressionable young minds.

The house wren is readily attracted to nest boxes. The nest box shown above was used for many years on our family farm in Iowa.

All that youthful interest, excitement, and fascination came from one little birdhouse. I still have that little wren house. It is a sentimental reminder of how my grandfather gently fostered an interest in wildlife among us grandchildren.

Since then I have been able to share my own interest in wildlife with thousands of people as supervisor of the DNR Nongame Wildlife Program. As I work with a variety of wildlife projects, I have never forgotten how important it is to stimulate an interest in wildlife in people when they are still young. And I have never forgotten the simple yet powerful lessons in nature that can be taught by the process of having parents or grandparents and children build and set out birdhouses.

This revised version of *Woodworking for Wildlife* incorporates new information that has evolved during the past 10 years so you can have the best chance possible of helping wildlife with your own nest-building efforts.

Building houses according to proper specifications, placing them in proper habitat, and maintaining the houses regularly can benefit both birds and mammals. If they are not built and maintained properly, they can become either "sparrow slums," remain unused, or actually become a death trap to nesting birds and mammals.

Nest boxes are becoming increasingly important as intensifying forest management and firewood cutting reduce the availability of natural cavities. Nest boxes are therefore helpful for many caity nesting species.

Although most people think of house wrens, eastern bluebirds, purple martins, and wood ducks as the primary occupants of houses, many other birds and mammals will occupy them. Birdhouses are usually built to simulate a natural cavity in a tree, and there are 40 species of birds in Minnesota that nest in tree holes. Many other birds and mammals will also adapt to wooden nest platforms if they have the opportunity.

Birdhouses are especially useful in areas that lack large, old, hollow trees for nesting. They can lessen competition by house sparrows and European starlings because natural cavities have entrance sizes that often admit both of these pest species. Nest boxes can be designed for some songbirds so that one or both pest species can be excluded by using small entrance holes.

Though this book was written primarily for Minnesota residents, these plans can be readily adopted across the United States and elsewhere.

Building nest boxes for wildlife is a great hobby whether you have an elaborate woodshop or simple hand tools.

Photo: Tim Smalley

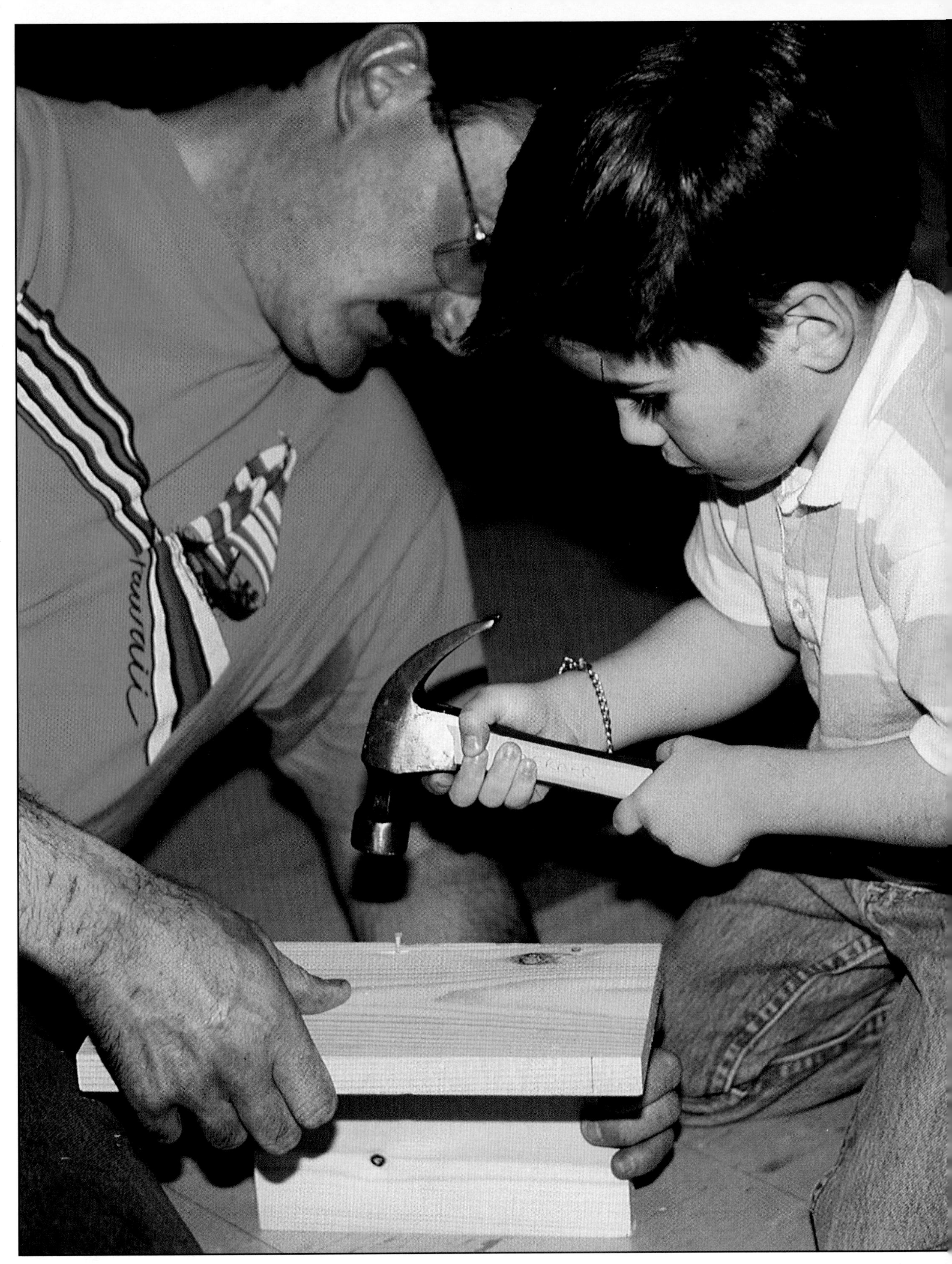

While it may be easier to "do it yourself," take the time to get young people involved with building nest boxes for wildlife.

Don't assume that woodworking for wildlife projects are just for little boys. Little girls enjoy helping wildlife too!

The house and platform instructions included here have been simplified to the greatest extent possible. Right-angle cuts are used wherever possible. Most patterns are one-board houses, including those in Figures 1, 3, 5, 6, 8, 9, 10, 11, 13, and 17.

This booklet is written in three habitat sections. The first section includes houses and platforms that are appropriate for use in back yards, small woodlots of deciduous trees (hardwoods), shelterbelts, pastures, and farmsteads. The second section includes houses and platforms for use in more extensive stands of deciduous or coniferous forest. The third section contains information for houses and platforms that can be used in lakes, rivers, marshes, and adjacent habitats. These three sections are followed by Part 4, which includes the designs for the structures mentioned in the text.

Please remember that placing and maintaining these nest structures does not eliminate the need for preserving and managing wildlife habitat or preserving snags (dead trees) for wildlife. Building, placing, and maintaining nest structures should be considered a technique for enhancing existing habitat and adding to our personal opportunities to see and enjoy wildlife.

This information is for everyone from children in nature classes to professional wildlife biologists. Included are directions on how to build 26 different structures that will accommodate 48 different species of wildlife.

There are many creative ways to use this information, such as in high school and middle school industrial arts classes or in workshops at state parks, county parks, or retirement homes.

These houses can be built and sold as fund-raising projects for sportsmen's clubs or youth or civic groups, and can be erected on the grounds of hospitals and retirement homes.

Try building some birdhouses as Christmas presents or birthday gifts. Watching the miracle of life unfold at a robin nesting shelf or wren house can be a thrilling experience for your family and friends.

Robin nesting shelf.

Info

■ *General House and Platform Instructions*

How to Build One-Board Birdhouse

Birdhouse Buyer's Guide

Birdhouse Pest Problems and Control

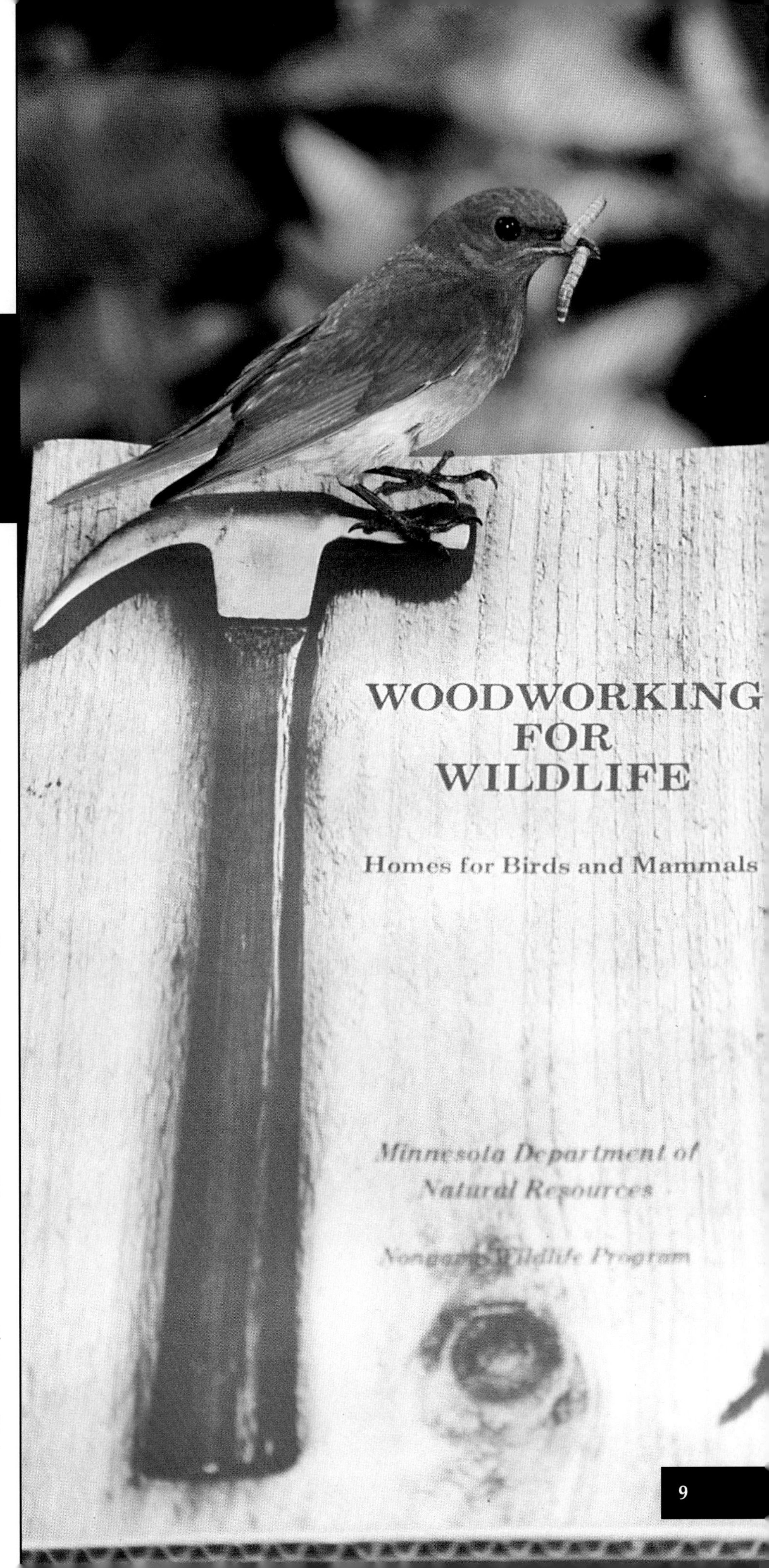

General House and Platform Instructions

Bird and mammal species each need different kinds of houses or platforms in different habitats. These general instructions will help you build and place houses and platforms for the most popular occupants of wildlife homes.

These general instructions apply to all plans.

Provide a hinged side or roof so your nest boxes can easily be checked and maintained. This is a Peterson bluebird house.

1. Do not make a box for "birds." Build it for a specific kind of bird or mammal. Different species have different house-size and entrance-hole requirements.

2. Provide a hinged side or roof so houses can be easily checked and cleaned out each year. Hinges should be rustproof. Duck and owl box roofs kept shut with a hook and eye can be opened by raccoons. It is much better to use several paired roofing nails with large heads on the side of the roof and on the upper edge of the side. Wire these paired nails together.

3. At least four 3/8 inch diameter drain holes should be drilled in the bottom of every house, except the Peterson bluebird house and the Helmeke wood duck nest box.

4. Although wren and flying squirrel houses can be suspended from an anchor point under an eave or tree limb, all other houses should be firmly attached to a support post, building, or tree. When you attach a nest box to a live tree, use lag bolts and washers. Then you can unscrew them to allow the tree to grow. This should be done every spring! Do not place bluebird houses on trees because cats and raccoons—bluebird predators—can easily climb trees!

5. Don't put perches on any birdhouses! Only house sparrows and European starlings prefer perches. If you have a house with a perch, remove the perch. A slab of wood with the bark attached should be placed horizontally under the entrance hole of a common merganser nest box to make it easier for them to land.

6. The top-front edge of a birdhouse should overhang at least two inches to help protect the entrance hole from wind-driven rain and to help keep cats from reaching in from above.

7. At least two 5/8-inch holes should be drilled near the top of the right and left sides of all birdhouses—except duck boxes—to provide ventilation. Providing adequate ventilation is very important for small birdhouses.

8. Cedar and redwood nest boxes should be made with wood screws, concrete coated or ring-shank nails. They won't allow the boards to loosen up. Galvanized nails easily loosen up as wood expands and contracts in extremely cold weather conditions.

9. The sides of a birdhouse should enclose the floorboard—don't nail them to the top of the floorboard. This keeps rain from seeping into the crack between sides and floor and then into the nest. Recess the floorboard 1/4 inch up from the bottom of the sides to help prevent deterioration caused by moisture.

10. Do not use tin cans, milk cartons, or metal for nests. There is not enough insulation. Metals heat up in direct sun, overheat the eggs, and kill the young. However, commercial martin houses made from aluminum are acceptable. Commercial plastic wood duck houses are also acceptable but should be placed in shady locations.

11. Wood is the best all-around material for houses. Boards 3/4 inch thick are the easiest to work with. Softwood such as pine is fine for smaller boxes, but cedar, redwood, or cypress should be used for the larger ones. Cedar is the all-around best choice. Pine or plywood can be used for duck boxes if they are treated on the outside of the box with wood preservative. Do **not** use wood treated with green preservative. The green copper-based preservative, when exposed to water, can produce poisonous vapors. A well-constructed house should last 10 to 15 years. The back should be coated with preservative several times because it is most prone to rotting. Do not paint, stain, or treat a box with creosote. If you must paint or stain, do not put **any** inside the house.

12. Purple martins, goldeneyes, mergansers, and wood ducks do not defend territories around their nests. Therefore, martins should be provided with "apartment type" houses. Duck and merganser boxes can be clustered in groups of two or four. Houses for other bird species should be spaced apart to reduce territorial conflicts. Bluebird houses need to be 100 yards apart.

13. Small animals such as mice and squirrels may take up residence in birdhouses. If not acceptable, remove the nests. Otherwise, you will probably need to put up additional houses to accommodate both the unexpected tenants and the desired wildlife species.

14. If wasps or bees take over a house, remove the wasp or bee nest and spray the interior with a disinfectant. Use extreme caution to avoid being stung. A can of aerosol insecticide may be necessary during this process for "self-defense." If an ant colony becomes established, place a commercial ant killer in an upside down pop bottle cap under the nest.

15. Blowfly eggs and larvae will sometimes become established in a bluebird nest. The larvae will suck blood from the young birds. If this occurs, lift up the nest with your fingers and gently tap the nest. The larvae will fall through the nest and can be removed from the bottom of the box. If the nest is heavily infested, remove the old nest and transfer the young to a new nest made out of soft grass. Then place the new nest back in the box.

16. When the nesting season is over, open the front or side of a songbird house and leave it that way during winter to prevent deer mice from nesting. Otherwise these mice may "defend" their box from returning songbirds in the spring by killing and eating songbirds that enter "their" box.

17. Be sure to allow for the width of the saw blade when marking a board.

18. Remember that the width and depth of lumber purchased at lumber yards is smaller than its standard description. For example, a 1" x 6" board is actually 3/4" x 5-1/2". A 2" x 4" is actually 1-1/2" x 3-1/2". The plans in this booklet utilize the actual dimensions of boards to make the most efficient use of wood. The dimensions in this book allow for 1" inch lumber that is actually 3/4" thick. (Caution: Some cedar boards are actually 7/8" or 1" thick. If you use these, you will need to reduce the dimensions of the floor piece to make it fit.)

19. Sawdust is **not** the best material for the bottom of a nest box for northern screech-owl, barred owl, northern saw-whet owl, boreal owl, American kestrel, wood duck, hooded merganser, common goldeneye, and common merganser! It tends to pack down when wet, and retains moisture. Wood chips from a chain saw or wood shavings are a better lining. They allow for better drainage.

20. The actual sizes of the entrance holes for all songbird, woodpecker, and squirrel nest boxes are shown in Figure 26 on page 109. The actual sizes of entrance holes for all duck, merganser, and raccoon nest boxes are shown in Figure 27 on page 110. These holes can be traced onto wood using carbon paper.

Young bluebirds.

How to Build a One-Board Birdhouse

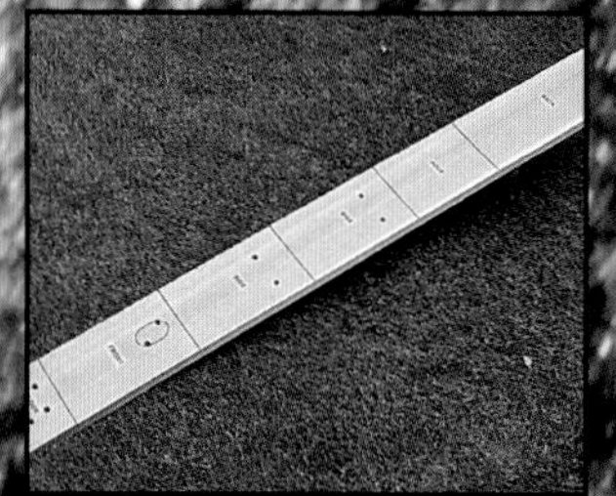

1. Select a board that is straight, with few knots, and without split ends. Cedar is best. Cedar will have one smooth side and one roughened side. Assemble the house so the roughened side faces outward.

2. Using a square, mark the board as indicated in Part 4. (pp. 79–108) Remember to allow for the width of the saw blade.

3. Drill the entrance hole, ventilation holes, and drainage holes before assembling the house.

4. Cut out the pieces as marked.

5. Cedar is prone to splitting, so drill the nail holes. Use a drill bit slightly smaller than the nail diameter. This is especially desirable if you are having young people assemble the nest boxes.

6. Vertically center the left side to the back of the nest box, drill two holes, and fasten with wood screws or ring-shank nails.

7. Fit the floor section into the box so it is 1/4 inch up from the bottom edge of the left side. Fasten the floor to the left side and back.

8. Fit the front section onto the box so the top and bottom edges are even with the left side.

9. Fasten the front to the floor and side.

10. Fasten the roof to the front, left side, and back.

11. Nail a quarter round along the top rear edge of the roof as a rain guard.

12. Using a square, mark a horizontal line about 1-1/2 inches down from the roof along the right side of the box. Since you will only be using two nails as your pivot points, this line will show where you must drill holes on the front and back so the side will tip out evenly.

13. Predrill the nail holes. Then insert the right side—this piece must be attached last. Before nailing, bring the side down about 1/8 inch so there is a small gap between the roof and the side. This makes it easier to open.

14. Drill one last hole at the lower front edge into the right side. This nail, partly nailed in, will be pulled out each time the nest box is checked.

15. The right side is pulled open from the bottom to inspect the box.

16. A complete one-board birdhouse!

Birdhouse Buyer's Guide

Buyer Beware—The Good, the Bad, and the Ugly

If you buy commercially made birdhouses, here are some tips on what to look for, and what to avoid.

1. Do **not** buy a wren, chickadee, tree swallow, or bluebird house with a perch.

2. The sides of a birdhouse should **enclose** the floor, or rain can readily seep into the nest.

3. Where the floor is properly enclosed by the sides, as shown here, the floor should be recessed upward at least a quarter inch to prevent rain from seeping in.

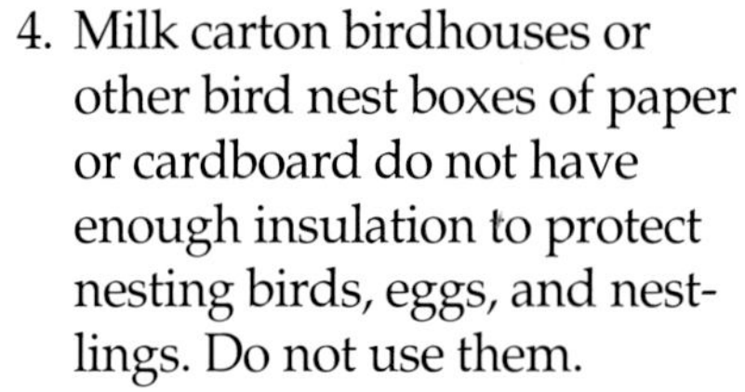

4. Milk carton birdhouses or other bird nest boxes of paper or cardboard do not have enough insulation to protect nesting birds, eggs, and nestlings. Do not use them.

5. Do not buy nest boxes that have been stapled together. They will not last more than a year or two. Look for nest boxes that are nailed or screwed together.

6. The entry hole on this wood duck box is too big. It will admit raccoons. Wood duck entry holes should be an oval 3" high and 4" wide.

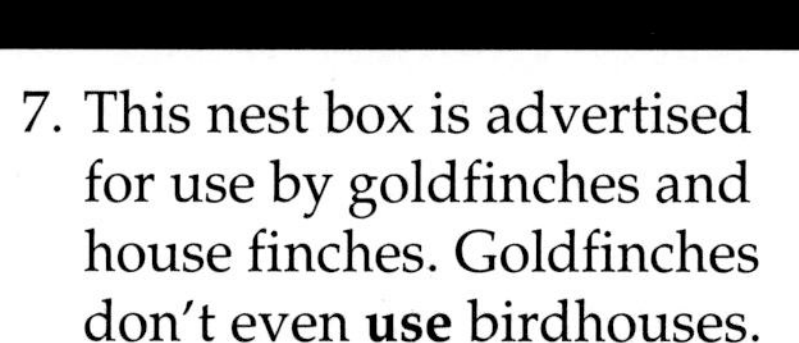

7. This nest box is advertised for use by goldfinches and house finches. Goldfinches don't even **use** birdhouses.

8. This bluebird house is designed to resemble the Peterson bluebird house, but it is not the Peterson design. The exact specifications of the Peterson bluebird house are shown in this book.

9. This nest box has been stapled shut. There is no way to open it to check the birds or to clean out the nest. Don't buy a sealed nest box. Nest boxes with removable floors are less desirable because you could dump out all the eggs while trying to check the nest.

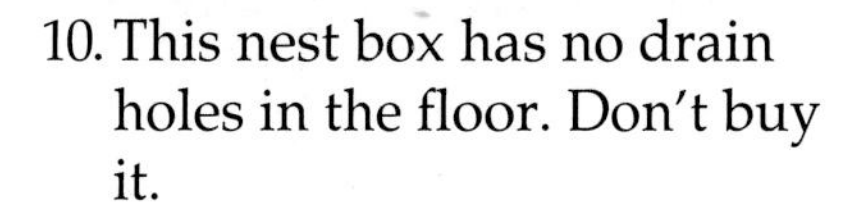

10. This nest box has no drain holes in the floor. Don't buy it.

Photo: Dr. Mike Zicus

11. This common goldeneye hen is attempting to use a metal nesting box, but is showing signs of extreme stress from the heat. Wooden boxes are a much better alternative because of better insulation.

Birdhouse Pest Problems and Control

Sparrow and Starling Problems and Control

One of the greatest challenges and frustrations that will face someone trying to provide nest boxes for wildlife is the problem faced by nest box competition from house sparrows and European starlings. These are nuisance exotic species that will kill or drive away native songbirds. They are not protected by state or federal law. There is no such thing as peaceful coexistence between house sparrows and bluebirds, chickadees, tree swallows, or house wrens. If house sparrows are successful in catching a female songbird in a nest box with its young, it will kill the whole family by pecking their skulls open.

Photo: Dick Peterson

The house sparrow can kill songbirds attempting to use your nest boxes.

House sparrows can enter any birdhouse with an entry hole of 1-1/4" diameter or greater. European starlings can enter any entrance hole larger than 1-1/2" diameter. These two species can be live-trapped but **should not** be released elsewhere. They will need to be caught and dispatched humanely. They can then be frozen and donated to a local raptor or wildlife rehabilitation center to feed crippled hawks or owls.

House sparrows can be caught in live traps like the Cedar Valley Live Trap. It is available from Orrin Tietz, 7441 100th St. Circle, Bloomington, MN 55438. This type of trap resets itself and can catch many sparrows in one day. The Cedar Valley Live Trap, and other live traps for sparrows, are also available from The Bird House, 5898 Omaha Ave. N., Stillwater, MN 55082. Phone: 612-439-1923.

The skull of this bluebird has been fractured by a house sparrow.

These young bluebirds were killed by house sparrow.

The Cedar Valley Live Trap is effective for removing house sparrows where they are a problem.

If sparrows move into a Peterson bluebird house, a removable sparrow trap front can be temporarily installed on the box to trap and remove the sparrow. If the nest is already in use, the female should be trapped within 20 minutes. In other types of nest boxes, if the sparrow nest already contains eggs, a mouse trap can be set over the eggs to catch the sparrow.

Photo: Dick Peterson

A house cat can devastate local songbird populations if allowed to roam free.

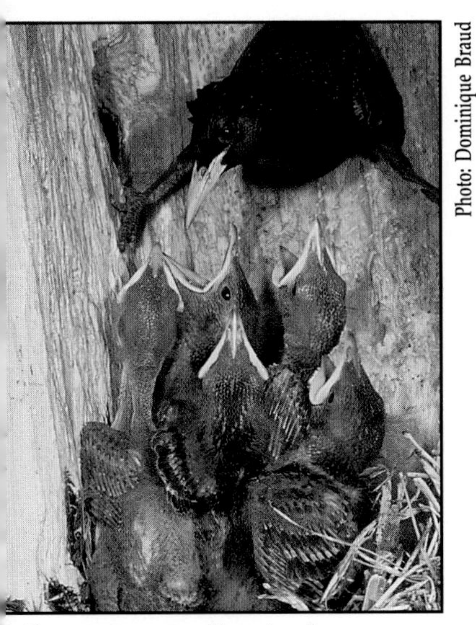

Photo: Dominique Braud

A European starling is shown here feeding its young.

House Cat and Raccoon Problems and Control

Two of the most significant mammalian predators of songbirds using nest boxes are house cats and raccoons. Both can devastate a bird nesting effort by killing adults and young.

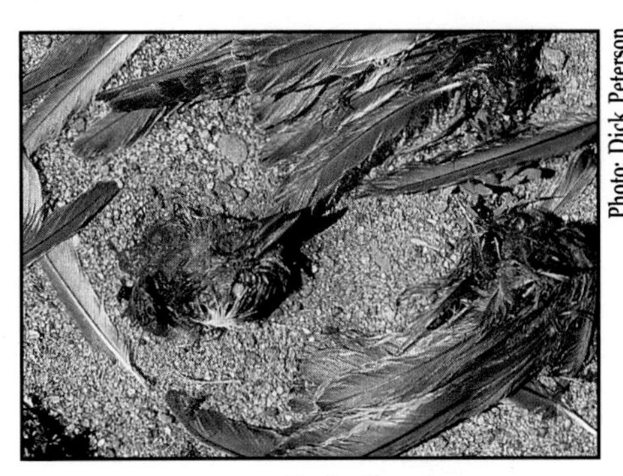

Photo: Dick Peterson

Only feathers remain where a cat has eaten a bluebird.

Starling nests may need to be routinely removed from kestrel and wood duck nest boxes.

Either sparrows or starlings can also be caught by hand by visiting the nest box after dark.

House sparrow eggs and nest.

Photo: Dick Peterson

A Noel coon guard can help prevent cats from entering nest boxes. See photo on next page.

A Noel coon guard is made from hardware cloth.

Photo: Dick Peterson

A sheet of tin or aluminum can be nailed around a tree or post below the nest box to reduce predation by mammals.

Raccoons are very intelligent mammals that quickly learn to raid nest boxes. A Noel coon guard protects this box from predation.

The Noel coon guard is a hardware cloth guard placed around the entry hole of the Peterson bluebird house, acting as a tunnel for the bluebird and a guard against predators. It is extremely effective in preventing raids by house cats and raccoons. It is available from The Bird House, 5898 Omaha Ave. N., Stillwater, MN 55082. Phone (612) 439-1923. Larger free-standing posts or trees can be covered with tin or aluminum sheets to prevent cats or raccoons from climbing them.

Another effective technique for preventing these mammals from reaching nests on steel posts or on concrete reinforcing rods (re-rods) used as posts is to smear the posts with axle grease. This grease is available in tubes from hardware stores. Cats and raccoons don't like to get grease in their fur.

Another alternative is to use a live-trap baited with an open can of sardines to catch feral house cats that are hunting on your property. Such cats can then be turned over to the local humane society.

Part 1

Nest boxes and platforms for use in back yards, urban areas, farmsteads, orchards, pastures, shelterbelts, and small deciduous woodlots

A pair of eastern bluebirds has selected a Peterson nest box for their nesting site.

Photo: H. Cruickshank/VIREO

The adaptable house wren is readily attracted to nest in a back yard.

House wren.

1. House Wren

Figure 1 (page 80)

The house wren is one of our most common and enjoyable backyard birds. Its beautiful bubbling songs are a joy to hear during the summer.

House wren nest boxes are likely to be used if they are 5 to 10 feet above the ground and located under the eave of a building or in a tree. This is the only kind of birdhouse that can be free-hanging from an eye-screw. All other birdhouses need to be firmly anchored. House wren holes are too small for sparrows or European starlings to use. Don't put a perch on the nest box. Perches invite sparrows to try to use the nest box. If you have a perch on a wren house, take it off.

The entrance hole for a wren house should be 1 inch in diameter. The 1-1/8-inch hole size shown in Figure 1 also allows use by chickadees, but not house sparrows.

House wrens generally nest in wooded, shrubby habitats. Their nests are characterized by twigs and the six to eight eggs are finely speckled with reddish spots. Sometimes wrens will take over the nest of a tree swallow, chickadee, or eastern bluebird after puncturing the eggs of the other birds with their bills.

As soon as one family of wrens leaves a house, clean it out so another brood of young ones can be raised.

2. White-breasted Nuthatch

Figure 1 (page 80)

The white-breasted nuthatch is well-known at winter bird feeders as it hangs upside down to eat suet and probe for insect larvae under the bark of trees. It will also nest in mature hardwood forests in habitat similar to that used by chickadees.

Nuthatches are not a common nest box occupant, but they will nest in houses placed for them in mature hardwood forest areas.

As soon as each brood of young leaves the nest box, clean it out so more birds can use it. Nuthatches need an entrance hole 1-1/4 inches in diameter. Since this also allows use by sparrows, use only in deep woods. Houses should be about 12 to 20 feet above the ground. This will also accomodate flying squirrels.

The white-breasted nuthatch is a w bird that will sometimes use a nest

Photo: Dominique Braud

The mourning dove usually lays two white eggs in a flimsy stick nest. A nesting cone like the one shown below can help ensure the survival of young after they hatch.

Photo: J. W. Heitke

3. Mourning Dove

Figure 2 (page 81)

Mourning doves are one of Minnesota's most abundant and adaptable birds. They do not nest in tree cavities or nest boxes, but they will use a simple, shallow cone of 1/4-inch or 1/2-inch mesh hardware cloth that is wired into the horizontal crotches of tree limbs. First, cut out a 12-inch-square piece of hardware cloth with tin snips. Then trim the square to form a circle 12 inches in diameter. You can also use composition asphalt shingles with the black side up. If you do, cut a 1-inch-diameter circle in the center of the cone to allow for drainage.

Next, cut out a pie-shaped wedge from the circle that is about 2-1/2 inches wide along the outer edge of the circle. Pull the two cut edges together and overlap them about 1 inch. Wire or staple the two edges together.

Place the nest cone in moderate shade in the crotch of a horizontal tree limb from 6 to to 16 feet above the ground. There should be open space around the nest cone for easy access by the doves. Use roofing nails, staples, or wire to securely fasten the nest in place. Bend back the cut edges of the cone so that the sharp points of wire do not stick out.

Dove nests are very simple structures made of twigs. They usually contain two white eggs. Mourning doves usually nest two or three times every summer. Sometimes they nest in old robin or grackle nests.

This simple and inexpensive nest cone is an excellent one for young people to make in nature classes.

4. Black-capped Chickadee

Figure 1 (page 80)

Photo: Dick Peterson

Fledgling black-capped chickadee.

The black-capped chickadee was selected as Minnesota's favorite bird during an informal survey conducted by the Department of Natural Resources. Many people enjoy these delightful birds at their feeders every winter but don't realize they will also nest in yards and woodlots with mature hardwood trees.

The house in Figure 1 will be used by black-capped chickadees if placed in the proper habitat—either mature hardwood shelterbelts and woodlots in agricultural areas or mature hardwood forests in other parts of the state. The house should be mounted 5 to 15 feet high with 40 to 60 percent sunlight. About an inch of sawdust should be placed in the bottom of the nest box. The chickadee needs an entrance hole 1-1/8 inch in diameter. This size entrance hole (shown in Figure 1) also allows use by wrens but not house sparrows.

Photo: Dick Peterson

The black-capped chickade is a welcome occupant of nest boxes. Their nest is m of greenish mosses and wil contain up to eight finely speckled eggs.

5. Chickadee Winter Roost Box

Figure 3 (page 82)

Although the main emphasis of this book is to provide nest boxes for wildlife, there are also some non-migratory bird species that use winter roost boxes. The black-capped chickadee is an example.

There are several differences between a nest box and a winter roost box. The entry hole of a winter roost box should be placed low on the front or side of the house so warmer air will rise and be trapped inside the box. A staggered arrangement of six 3/8-inch or 1/2-inch diameter, 6-inch-long birch dowels should be inserted into one side of the roost box to provide perching sites. The dowels should be roughened with course sandpaper. The dowels should be horizontal and placed in the upper half of the box. To make the box more airtight under the roof section, a 9-1/4" x 7-3/4" x 1" piece of styrofoam or beadboard wall insulation should be glued or fastened to the bottom of the roof section to help seal the top against heat loss.

The entrance hole should be 1-1/2 inches above the floor section and 1-1/8 inches in diameter. If other species are desired, make the hole 2 to 2-1/2 inches in diameter.

Also, tack a 4" x 8" piece of screendoor screen to the inside back section of the box to make it easier for the birds to grip the wall as they flutter up and down to their roosting places.

This young tree swallow is ready for its first flight from the nest box.

6. Tree Swallow

Figures 4b and 5 (Pages 84 and 86)

The tree swallow has a snow white breast and beautiful iridescent blue-green-black back. It eats flying insects, and nests in the same type of house used by bluebirds.

Tree swallows and eastern bluebirds often nest in the same areas. If there is a shortage of nest boxes, bluebirds and tree swallows will fight over nesting sites. The best way to eliminate this competition is to "pair" two nest boxes 25 feet apart. One box can be occupied by bluebirds and the other by tree swallows. If you are trying to maximize tree swallow production in good swallow habitat—like around the margin of a marsh or pond—single nest boxes can be set up at 50-foot intervals.

Photo: Dick Peterson

The tree swallow is distinguished by its iridescent bluish black back and white belly.

Bluebird chicks beg for food. Notice how this nest is lined with fine grass and contains no droppings from the chicks. The tree swallow nest shown below has feather lining that makes it easy to distinguish from bluebird nes

Nest boxes should be placed so the entrance hole faces east. The nest boxes should be about 4 feet above the ground. Tree swallows are especially abundant near water.

Their nests are often characterized by a feather lining. The eggs are white. The houses should be ready by May 1, and should be cleaned out as soon as the young leave. They generally nest only once each year, but cleaning out the box helps make room for a second brood of bluebirds.

Tree swallow eggs are white and the nest is lined with feathers.

Photo: Dick Peterson

7. Eastern Bluebird

Figures 4b and 5 (Pages 84, 86)

Eastern bluebirds are one of the most popular of native songbirds. Their brilliant blue color, delightful songs, clean habits, and family devotion have long provided happiness and inspiration to people.

Ideal bluebird habitat is comprised of mixed hardwood forests and grasslands. The grassy areas may be meadows, oak savannahs, pastures, yards, cemeteries, golf courses, highway rights of way, or prairies. It is best if the grass is short or sparse. Mowed or grazed areas provide good habitat. There should be either power lines, fenceposts, or scattered trees in the grassy areas to provide feeding perches. Bluebirds will sometimes nest in the back yards of homes in rural areas or on the fringe of urban areas. Normally they nest in rural areas away from the farmstead sites because competition with house sparrows is often too great near the farm buildings. You can give bluebirds an edge in such areas by trapping and removing house sparrows.

Bluebird nests are neat, cup-shaped structures made of fine grass. Usually there are five pale blue eggs in a clutch. For more details, see the book: *Bluebirds in the Upper Midwest,* by Dorene H. Scriven.

The Peterson bluebird house shown in Figure 4b is the best type of bluebird house. It is relatively safe for bluebirds and is easily checked and cleaned.

Eastern bluebird.

Photo: Dick Peterson

A bluebird nest normally contains five to six pale blue eggs.

A nestling bluebird begs for food.

Photo: Dick Peterson

Eastern bluebirds are devoted parents that feed their young from dawn to dusk.

The most successful bluebird houses

This 18-d
bluebird i
for its firs

checked weekly from April through August. Checking allows prompt response to any problems that occur.

This bluebird has just completed its first flight.

The eastern bluebird eats a variety of small insects and caterpillars.

The seven parts of this house are assembled in this order: First, the inner roof is toe-nailed to the top front edge of the back. Second, the floor is toe-nailed to the back 10-1/2 inches below the top. Toe-nailing may be easier to do if you hot-glue the pieces together first. Third, one side is nailed to the resulting frame. Then the other side is nailed to the frame. Next the swing-down front is fastened by nailing one nail to each side of the base. A third nail is pounded part-way into the side near the entrance hole. This is pulled out each time the house is checked. Finally the outer roof is nailed on top. This top serves primarily as a cat guard. Figure 4a shows the detail necessary to mass produce the Peterson bluebird house.

A one-board bluebird house (Figure 5) is much easier to build than the Peterson house and is included here for the benefit of young people or for adults who do not have access to table saws or radial arm saws. This type of house is more vulnerable to predation by house cats so it is best used on free-standing posts that have tin or aluminum sheets stapled around the support post. The post can also be smeared with axle grease to prevent cats and raccoons from climbing the post. Some people feel that sparrow use in the one-board house can be diminished by cutting a 3-inch-diameter hole in the roof and covering the hole with 1/4- or 1/2-inch hardware cloth mesh. Bluebirds don't seem to mind the "sunroof" but sparrows may be discouraged by it. Such open top nests need to be covered in March and April to avoid mortality during spring ice storms.

Either the Peterson or one-board bluebird houses should be placed 5 to 6 feet above the ground and spaced about 100 yards apart. The entrance hole should face north, east, or northeast to prevent sunlight from shining into the hole and overheating the box interior. A bluebird trail consists of five or more houses placed along a road or fenceline. The houses should be ready by late March and should be checked every seven to 10 days from late March until mid-August. A nest should be removed as soon as a brood leaves its nest box. This allows a second brood to be raised.

To decrease or eliminate nest box competition from tree swallows, it is best to pair nest boxes 25 feet apart. Then place the next pair of houses 100 yards away. Bluebirds will normally occupy one nest box and the tree swallows will nest in the other box without fighting the bluebirds. (Pairing does not reduce competition from house sparrows.)

To prevent predation by raccoons in Peterson nest boxes, the Noel raccoon guard is extremely effective (see page 18). This guard is a 1/2-inch-mesh hardware cloth guard that is stapled to the front of the birdhouse.

If house wrens fill a bluebird house with sticks, the nest box is probably too close to woods or

Bluebirds in your back yard can provide hours of enjoyment as you watch them raise a family in the nest box you built for them.

brushy areas. Try moving the post another 20 to 25 feet out into the open.

Sparrows can be trapped and removed from the Peterson bluebird house by using a sparrow-trap front that is available from Dave Ahlgren, 12989 Otchipwe Ave. N., Stillwater, MN 55082; or from The Bird House, 5898 Omaha Ave. N., Stillwater, MN 55082. The Noel raccoon guard and Peterson bluebird houses are also available from these suppliers.

Bottoms up! A bluebird feeds its young.

Note: house finches are a relatively new nesting species in Minnesota and they may nest in bluebird houses. The Minnesota Department of Natural Resources is interested in such nest records.

Photo: Dick Peterson

The American robin is among the most common of backyard birds.

8. American Robin

Figure 6 (page 87)

One of Minnesota's most enjoyable backyard bird species is the American robin. It is a welcome sight in the spring, its song is beautiful, and it provides great enjoyment for people as it raises its young each summer. The grassy nest is lined inside with mud. A typical robin's nest will have 5 bright blue eggs.

A newly fledged robin visits a backyard patio.

Robins are not as easy to attract to nesting shelves as are phoebes. On buildings, they show a preference for nesting on shelves in sheltered sites under the eaves or soffits, and sometimes over light fixtures.

A robin nesting shelf can be placed on a wall by a window where the robin family can be easily seen. The nesting shelf can also be placed on the trunk of a tree about 6 to 10 feet above the ground. The nesting shelf can be left unpainted, or it can be painted an earth tone. The asphalt composition shingle nesting cone described for mourning doves may also be used by robins.

Remove the robin's nest after the young leave because robins build a new nest each year.

This site above a light fixture is typical of the places chosen by robins for nesting.

9. Barn Swallows

Figure 6 (page 87)

Barn swallows are a common inhabitant of farmsteads where they frequently nest on the rafters of barns or other outbuildings. Their mud nests are usually stuck onto the sides of rough-sawn rafters. These beautiful birds eat flying insects and are characterized by iridescent bluish-black backs, reddish breasts, and deeply forked tails.

Barn swallows will also use the nesting box illustrated in Figure 6. Sometimes barn swallows are a nuisance because they nest over light fixtures in doorways. Then they defend their territory against people trying to pass

These young barn swallows are spending their first night out of the nest.

10. Eastern Phoebe

Figure 6 (page 87)

The eastern phoebe is a small gray songbird that usually feeds on insects while flying over water. Phoebes sit on low branches overhanging the water of a pond or creek; then make a short abrupt flight out over the water to catch insects. They are one of the first birds to return in the spring.

Photo: C.H. Greenewalt/VIREO

Phoebes often build their nests on nesting shelves under the eaves of lake homes or cabins. The delicate nest is a beautiful cup-shaped structure made of mosses and lichens. The phoebe's call is a distinctive buzz-like "free-bee."

The eastern phoebe will readily use nest shelves on buildings near lakes or rivers.

Photo: D.B. Pettingill/VIREO

Barn swallow at its nest.

through the doorway. To solve this problem, staple a small piece of clear plastic, like sheeting above the light fixture after knocking down the old nest. The nest should only be removed after the young have fledged. The plastic will prevent mud from sticking to the wall. Then place a nesting shelf nearby on the house or garage wall so it is at least 10 or 20 feet from the doorway.

11. Purple Martin

Figure 7 (page 88-89)

Attracting purple martins is the ultimate challenge to a backyard bird enthusiast. Some people will put up a martin house in the spring and attract martins with relative ease. Other people may maintain martin houses for years in apparently good habitat, with no luck attracting them.

The purple martin is the largest member of the swallow family. It eats flying insects. Males are glossy black with purple iridescence. The markings of the female are somewhat duller.

Photo: Pam Perry

A purple martin's house should be at least 30 feet from trees. It should be at least 8 to 10 feet high. Martins eat large numbers of day-flying insects.

The wooden purple martin house design shown here should be modified to add a 1/2-inch-diameter birch dowel "fence" that is 2 inches high around the balcony to prevent young martins from falling to the ground. If they fall out of the house, they will not be fed by their parents.

Photo: E.S. Morton/VIREO

Purple martins will use aluminum or wooden nest boxes.

Another important new feature that must be added to martin houses is a set of partitions to separate the balcony sections between entrance holes. Otherwise, older, more mobile chicks can leave their nest and enter another nest where martin chicks are smaller. They will outcompete the smaller chicks for food and the smaller chicks can die.

Following is an itemized list of instructions for making this purple martin house.

Note: This unit is held together by a threaded rod extending from the underside of the 1" x 2" base frame through the center of the chimney. The nut at the base of the rod must be secured so it cannot turn and cannot fall off. One way to do this is to weld a 1-inch washer and the nut to the rod. Notch or drill a small hole in the washer and secure with a small nail to the base board.

1. Mark all pieces on plywood sheet, then cut them out. Make four 1" x 1" x 5-7/8" corner blocks and eight 1" x 1" x 2" blocks to position the parts.

2. Cut out and assemble base from 1" x 2". Use 7d galvanized siding nails. Attach floor piece to base with glue and 1" or 1-1/4" nails. You can increase the ventilation in a martin house by drilling 1-1/4" vent holes in the center of each room partition and stapling 1/4 inch hardware cloth over the hole. You can also create a ventilation hole in the floor of each room by drilling a 1-1/4" hole in the inside corner of each room and stapling 1/4 inch mesh hardware cloth over each hole.

3. Assemble the sides, alternating three hole and one hole pieces. Use glue and 1 inch nails or 3/4-inch No. 6 flat-head wood screws. Use three at each end of each piece.

4. Position first-story sides on base piece. Mark position for each 1" x 1" x 2" block to hold side in position. Attach blocks to floor with glue and two 1 inch nails or 3/4 inch No. 6 flat-head wood screws. Place completed sides in position on floor. Insert partitions. Position ceiling and mark for the location of 1" x 1" x 2" blocks near corners on the underside. Attach the blocks. (Remember that the entrance holes **must** be 1 inch above the floor—so don't install the walls upside down or the holes will be too high off the floor.)

5. Place ceiling in position.

6. Glue pairs of end roof supports together to form gable ends 1/2 inch thick. Attach screen. Position and mark. Glue the two center roof supports together to make it 1/2 inch thick. It will be positioned adjacent to the threaded rod going up through the exact center of the house. Attach these pieces to the ceiling with glue and nails or flat-head wood screws from the underside. Attach roof sides with glue and nails or screws.

7. Make chimney from a piece of 2" x 2". Cut V-notch on end to fit roof. Have it extend 2-1/2 inches above roof peak. Drill 1/4 inch hole in chimney and roof for rod. Nail chimney in place. Insert rod and tighten up.

8. Drill hole in top of pole to accommodate nut on lower end of threaded rod.

9. Use 1/2-inch-diameter maple dowels to make a fence about 2 inches high on each balcony. Pieces of wood 1" x 1" x 3" may be used as the corner posts of this railing.

Photo: Dan Engel

This newly assembled martin house is ready for painting.

Mounting

Use four 4" x 5" shelf brackets with 1/4" or 3/16" x 1-1/2" round head stove bolts and 1-inch No. 8 flat-head wood screws to attach to pole.

Note: Additional stories may be added if desired. One ceiling unit, four-sides, four-room partitions, eight 1" x 1" 2" blocks, and four 1" x 1" x 5-7/8" corner blocks will be needed for each additional story.

Do not paint the interior of the house. Lightweight roofing paper makes an efficient roof covering. When painting the house, use aluminum paint on the roofing paper before painting it white. This seals in the black tar of the paper.

Commercially made aluminum houses are acceptable if they are well-ventilated, have at least six compartments, with each compartment at least 6" x 6" x 6" in size. The entrance holes should be 2-1/4 inches in diameter and the bottom of the holes should be 1 inch above the floor.

Purple martins arrive in southern Minnesota from about April 15 to April 20. As soon as the first martins, or "scouts," are seen, remove entrance covers from the martin house. The covers are used to keep sparrows and starlings out during the winter. If a cold spell hits after martins arrive, insects will die and martins can starve. To help, place crushed egg shells on a flat, elevated surface near the martin house. Another special inducement for the martins is a 1' x 2' area of soaked, unsodded earth, which provides them with a "mud puddle" for a water supply.

Purple martin houses should be placed in an open area where the birds have clear access from all sides. The house should be at least 30 feet away from trees. Martins seem to prefer sites where utility wires are nearby for perching. Houses near open water like lakes may have added appeal but this is not essential. Martin houses should be painted white or a light color to reflect the sun's heat.

Some people suggest placing purple martin houses very high—from 12 to 18 feet. However, other people have good success placing the house on a 4" x 4" cedar post no more than 8 to 10 feet high so it is easier to maintain during the summer with a step ladder. Try using a 14-foot-long 4" x 4" cedar post. Set it 4 feet deep in the ground and secure the base by pouring a small batch of concrete in the post hole before filling the post hole. Then you can check the house easily with a ladder.

A martin house can be taken down, cleaned, and stored at the end of summer, or the entrances should be covered as soon as the martins leave in late August to early September. If a martin house is left up, the nesting cavities still need to be cleaned out.

Purple martin house.

Purple martin eggs are white.

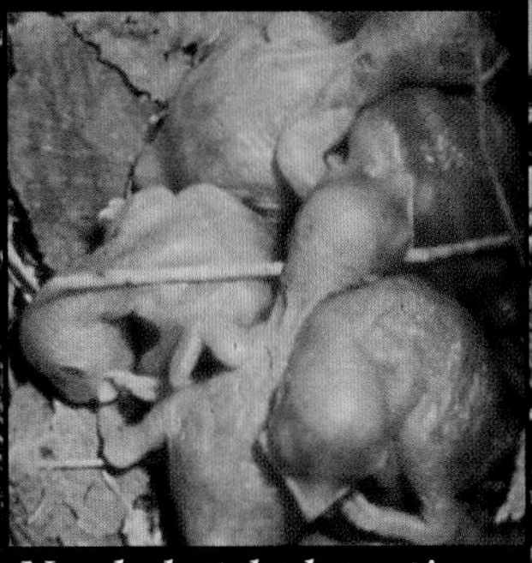

Newly hatched martin chicks.

Week-old chicks.

Two week-old chicks.

Inset Photos: Ted Johnson

More Tips for Attracting Purple Martins

Here are several additional tips to enhance the possibilities of attracting purple martins:

1. You **cannot** have purple martins and house sparrows because the sparrow is the martin's worst enemy. The best way to control sparrows is to trap them with the elevator-type sparrow trap. See page 16 on sparrow control for more details.

2. In the spring when putting up a martin house, place a handful of sawdust in each compartment.

3. Put a pinch of 1 percent rotenone powder on top of the sawdust. The rotenone keeps out and kills lice and red mites, which would otherwise kill or harm the young martins.

4. Spread alfalfa stems broken into 4 or 5 inch lengths on a bare spot near the house so the martins can use it for nesting material.

5. During the period when the young birds are being fed by the parents, spread crushed egg shells on a bare spot near the martin house. This provides calcium for the young birds. You can probably get lots of these from a nearby restaurant.

6. To keep sparrows under control, pull their nests out of the martin house with a wire hook. Do this in mid-afternoon when most of the martins are at a pond or river for bathing or feeding.

7. Make sure the bottom of the compartment entrance holes are no more than 1 inch above the floor. This allows for the young birds to get in and out to try their wings before they are ready to fly.

8. Martins love lots of high perches! You can accommodate them by erecting an old TV antenna near their house on a separate pole, or by stretching several cords between trees or buildings so the cords pass within several feet of the martin house.

9. If you are fortunate enough to own a lakeshore lot, your best site for a martin house is probably over the water at the end of your dock. Martin houses in such locations have a very high occupancy rate.

These recommendations are offered by Mr. A.J. Boersma of Sioux Center, Iowa. He has maintained large colonies of martins for more than 50 years. He also suggests placing the house 8 to 10 feet high on a solid post rather than using tall, hinged posts. The hinges tend to break down with extended use. He also stresses the importance of adequate ventilation within the house. This is done by drilling 1-1/4-inch-diameter air holes between compartments and providing an open air shaft in the center compartment of the house up to the "attic."

The purple martin house design offered here is derived from the excellent publication *Shelves, Houses, and Feeders for Birds and Squirrels* by G. Barquest, S. Craven, and R. Ellarson, published by the University of Wisconsin Extension Service.

Photo: J.R. Woodward/VIREO

The northern flicker is primarily a ground-foraging woodpecker that searches for ants and other terrestrial insects. The naked young give little indication what they will look like as adults.

Photo: Dick Peterson

12. Northern Flicker

Figure 8 (page 90)

Northern flickers are a very common member of the woodpecker family. They frequently nest in farm groves, orchards, woodlots, and in urban areas. Unlike most other woodpeckers, flickers usually forage for ants and grubs on the ground, in crop fields, and in grassy meadows and yards.

The secret of success in attracting flickers is to use 1-1/2 inch-thick boards for nest boxes and to fill the interior of the box all the way to the top with sawdust. Tamp in the sawdust before April 1 so the box is ready when the flickers arrive. This house should have a hinged roof to facilitate filling it with sawdust. The filled box simulates a dead tree with soft heartwood. Since the northern flicker is a "primary excavator," it will start at the entrance hole that is provided and throw out sawdust until a suitable cavity is created. Since this box remains filled with sawdust if not used, sparrows and starlings are not a problem. The entrance hole should be 2-1/2 inches in diameter.

This brilliant nest box idea was developed by Mr. A.J. Boersma of Sioux Center, Iowa.

13. Bats

Figure 9 and 10 (Pages 91 and 92)

Who in the world would think of building a house for bats? The idea sounds farfetched. Once bats are understood, however, their desirable qualities exceed even those of the popular purple martin. For example, some people claim that purple martins eat up to a thousand mosquitoes per day. Other people dispute that total, saying that the daily total of mosquitoes is much lower because martins don't actively feed when mosquitoes are most active. In contrast, bats do. A single, big brown bat can eat 3,000 to 7,000 insects each night! Many of those insects are mosquitoes. And a big brown bat can live up to 19 years. Bats are also devoted parents.

Photo: T. Simmons/American Society of Mammalogists

Big brown bats may live in caves, buildings, or nest boxes.

Expectant mother bats join together in "nursery" colonies where hundreds or thousands congregate to raise their young. Mother bats help each other with rearing young, and each female recognizes her own young. The big brown bat raises just one young per year. Males cooperate during this reproductive phase by either bringing food to their mates or leaving the maternity cave to reduce competition for limited food supplies—depending on the species.

Since bats are such an important form of natural control for insect pests like mosquitoes, it is in our own best interest to perpetuate them. This is already being done in much of Europe where bats are totally protected and where people build "bat houses" much like we build martin houses. Figure 9 shows a bat house design developed by DNR Area Wildlife Manager Earl Johnson of Detroit Lakes, Minn. Figure 10 shows a smaller style bat house that also works well.

Building and placing bat houses is a great way to provide for natural control of insect pests like mosquitoes.

The most likely occupants of bat houses are the big brown bat and little brown bat. The most critical dimension is the 1-inch-width of the entry space. All inner surfaces must be roughened with a chisel or saw cuts to permit bats to climb on them with ease. Rough outer surfaces are also preferred.

Daytime temperatures in the bat house must be very hot—about 80 to 90 degrees. One way to achieve this is to cover the bat house on top and extending a couple inches down the sides with two or more layers of tar paper. The dark color of the tar paper absorbs heat from the sun and helps protect bats from the rain. The tar paper can be stapled to the box. Another alternative is to paint the bat house black so it absorbs heat from the sunlight.

Bat houses should be securely fastened to a tree trunk or the side of a building roughly 12 to 15 feet above the ground. Preferably they should be on the east side of the house or tree where they will receive the morning sun but will be shaded during the afternoon. Bats also seem to prefer sites that are protected from the wind.

The best habitat for bat houses is near rivers, lakes, bogs, or marshes where insect populations are high. The closer bat houses are to such places the greater the probability of being used. Those located more than a half mile from these habitats have a low probability of being used.

Bat houses should be placed by early April, but it may take a year or two for bats to find the house. Once used, they do not need to be cleaned. Chances of occupancy are better if bats already live in nearby buildings.

Another technique that may work to attract bats is to nail a 2-foot-wide piece of tar paper around a tree trunk. Nail the tar paper around the top edge, like a tight-fitting skirt. This will prevent water from leaking under the tar paper from above. The bats will enter from below and can cling to the bark of the tree. To regulate their body temperature they can move laterally around the tree trunk as the sun moves during the day.

Sometimes bats create severe problems for people by establishing huge colonies in the attics of homes. The best way to solve this problem is to hire a carpenter **in the winter** to exclude bats at the holes where they enter the house. Since most bats migrate, it is possible to exclude the bats while they are not present.

It is a good idea to set up an alternative bat roost box when you bat-proof your home.

A Missouri-style bat house is desirable for large bat concentrations. Such houses may be useful at state parks or on other public park and wildlife lands where large numbers of bats may be causing problems in residences or outbuildings. One of these bat houses has been built at the DNR Area Fisheries Headquarters at Detroit Lakes, Minn., to help solve a bat problem at the manager's residence. It now houses a nursery colony of more than 100 bats! A blueprint for the Missouri-style bat house is available by writing to the DNR Nongame Wildlife Program, Box 7, 500 Lafayette Road, St. Paul, MN 55155.

If you try placing a bat house or tar paper shelter, send the results of your efforts to the DNR Nongame Wildlife Program, Box 7, 500 Lafayette Road, St. Paul, MN 55155.

This information on bat houses has been provided by Dr. Merlin D. Tuttle, Joan Galli and Earl Johnson.

Missouri-style bat house.

14. Burrowing Owl

Figure 11 (page 93)

The endangered burrowing owl seems an unlikely candidate for a nest box because it nests underground. However, the lack of adequate burrow sites may be a limiting factor in otherwise suitable habitat. The burrowing owl is extremely rare in Minnesota, but does occasionally nest in western counties in cattle pastures and amid colonies of Richardson's ground squirrels ("flickertails"). Flickertails usually occur in heavily grazed pastures and their colonies resemble prairie dog towns. Owls use the burrows for their nests.

The nesting tunnel and box shown in Figure 11 will be readily used by burrowing owls if they are in the vicinity. This type of nesting tunnel was successfully used by burrowing owls in southwestern Minnesota in 1990. The tunnels in pastures may need to be constructed of 1-1/2-inch-thick lumber to avoid collapsing under the weight of cattle and horses that may step on the nest boxes. Otherwise, dimensions shown in the diagram are acceptable.

Corrugated plastic tile or flexible 8-inch-diameter septic tank tubing can also be used instead of the wooden tunnel. This tubing is then connected to the nest box.

This burrow consists of a nest chamber that is 12" x 12" x 8" deep. It is made of warp-resistant plywood. The top is a removable

Nest tunnel shown in place before covering with dirt.

Covered tunnel should have an entrance that looks like a badger den.

Home Sweet Home!

Inset Photos: John Schladweiler

lid so the young can be checked. The tunnel connecting the nesting chamber to the entrance is about 6 feet long with a right-angle turn about 4 feet from the entrance. The bottom of this structure is open to provide a dirt floor. The whole burrow is buried horizontally to a depth of 6 inches to provide enough dirt over the nesting chamber for insulation. A burrow usually needs to be renovated before each nesting season begins in mid-May. Place this tunnel on a relatively high and well-drained site to prevent drowning of the owls during heavy rains.

It is probably advantageous to have a mound of dirt around the tunnel entrance to simulate the entrance of a badger den. This helps attract the attention of burrowing owls.

This technique was first tried in California in 1975. Burrowing owls moved into 20 of 30 tunnels that were provided.

This idea is derived from C.T. Collins and R.E. Landry, 1977, "Artificial Nest Burrows for Burrowing Owls," *North American Bird Bander,* 2(4):151-154.

Should any owls use the boxes, contact the DNR Regional Nongame Specialist, Box 756, Highway 15 S., New Ulm, MN 56073. Phone: 507-359-6000.

15. Gray and Fox Squirrels

Figure 13 (page 95)

Gray and fox squirrels readily adapt to nest boxes in back yards, woodlots, and farm groves. Gray squirrels tend to be found more in urban areas and in larger stands of hardwood forest in southeastern, east-central and central Minnesota. Fox squirrels are found more commonly in farmsteads, river bottoms, and woodlots of western and southwestern Minnesota.

A squirrel nest box is identical to the screech-owl box shown in Figure 13, except for the location of the entrance hole and the ventilation holes. A 3-inch-diameter entrance is placed to the upper rear portion of one side. It is centered 3-1/2 inches from the top and 2-1/2 inches from the back edge. Ventilation holes are drilled into the side opposite the entrance.

A 4-inch-long piece of 2" x 2" can be nailed horizontally inside the nest box and 4 inches below the entrance hole as a perch for the squirrels to stand on while peering out of the entrance hole.

Photo: Dick Peterson

Young gray squirrels.

Houses should be placed in trees that are at least 10 inches in diameter. They should be at least 15 feet above the ground. The entrance hole should face either east or south to be downwind from prevailing winter winds. A squirrel nest box can be made more enticing to squirrels by filling it half full of dry leaves. To attach the box to the tree, use a lag bolt and washer at both the top and bottom of the back piece. Lag bolts must be loosened annually to allow for tree growth. Wire should not be used because it can girdle the tree. Boxes are most heavily used in the winter, so new boxes should be set out in the fall. It is not necessary to clean out squirrel nest boxes.

One or two squirrel boxes per acre in a woodland are usually sufficient to maintain a maximum squirrel population.

Photo: Dr. Bruce Edinger

Raccoon.

16. Raccoon

Figure 17 (page 99)

The raccoon is a common mammal across most of Minnesota except in the far northeastern coniferous forests. Most nest box projects are designed to exclude use or predation by raccoons. If someone wishes to provide a box that can be used by raccoons, however, the design in Figure 17 is appropriate. The entrance hole should be 4-1/2 inches in diameter and face east or south so it is sheltered from prevailing winter winds. The box should be placed on live or dead trees at a height of 10-to-20 feet. The tree should be at least 12 inches in diameter.

17. Woodland Deer Mouse and White-footed Mouse

Figure 1 (page 80)

The woodland deer mouse and white-footed mouse are frequent occupants of nest boxes placed for house wrens, chickadees, and bluebirds. They are distinctively marked by brown or grayish backs, white bellies, long tails, and very prominent eyes. While they may occasionally be a nuisance if they take up residence in a cabin, they are both rather appealing and interesting native mammal species.

Some people intentionally place nest boxes for these two native mouse species on fence posts along fencelines near their northern cabins or at nature centers. A wren house as shown in Figure 1 is appropriate for use by these two mice. Nest boxes should be on posts about 3 or 4 feet above the ground.

As the mice raise their families they can provide a constant source of enjoyment and fascination for children who may occasionally open the side of the box and peek at the bug-eyed occupants within. Mice will winter in these boxes, so the entry hole should face east or southeast to avoid prevailing northwest winds.

These mice do carry deer ticks that are a carrier of Lyme disease, so be careful to avoid coming in contact with these ticks while checking these nest boxes.

Photo: Gregory K. Scott

The woodland deer mouse and white-footed mouse are frequent occupants of small nest boxes.

The only problem with mouse use in nest boxes is that if birds return to a songbird nest box in the spring and enter a box occupied by deer mice or white-footed mice, the mice might kill and eat the birds in order to defend their box. Nest boxes for house wrens, chickadees, nuthatches, tree swallows, bluebirds and other small songbirds should therefore be left **open** in the winter to prevent their use by wintering deer mice and white-footed mice. Boxes intended for these mice should be left closed in the winter.

The American kestrel, our smallest falcon, readily uses nest boxes. This one is a male.

18. American Kestrel

Figure 13 (page 95)

The American kestrel is our smallest falcon and is abundant in agricultural areas characterized by scattered woodlots, scattered trees, shelterbelts, meadows, highway rights of way, pastures, and hay fields. This species is valuable because of the large numbers of rodents and insects eaten. Kestrels are frequently seen sitting on powerlines along highways or hovering above the grassy roadside ditches in search of their prey. An adult kestrel is about the size of a grackle.

Iowa has a program in which kestrel nest boxes are placed on the back of information signs along Interstate Highway 35. The boxes are predator proof because the steel posts supporting the signs can't be climbed by cats or raccoons. The grassy interstate right-of-way is ideal habitat for kestrels. The boxes are strapped to the vertical sign posts with steel bands by using a steel banding tool that is normally used for strapping steel bands around freight.

In southern Minnesota and northern Iowa, about 40 to 60 percent of all kestrel boxes placed by the Iowa and Minnesota DNR are used by kestrels.

The nest box shown in Figure 13 is ideal for kestrels. Place the box in orchards or relatively open country on a tree or a free-standing post that is 10 to 30 feet high. The tree or post should have a sheet of tin or aluminum nailed or stapled around it, under the box, to prevent squirrels from using the box. The nest hole should be 3 inches in diameter and preferably face south or west. About 2 to 3 inches of wood chips should be placed in the bottom of the box. Grassy habitat should be in the vicinity to provide hunting habitat for the kestrels. Kestrel boxes should be spaced one-half mile from each other.

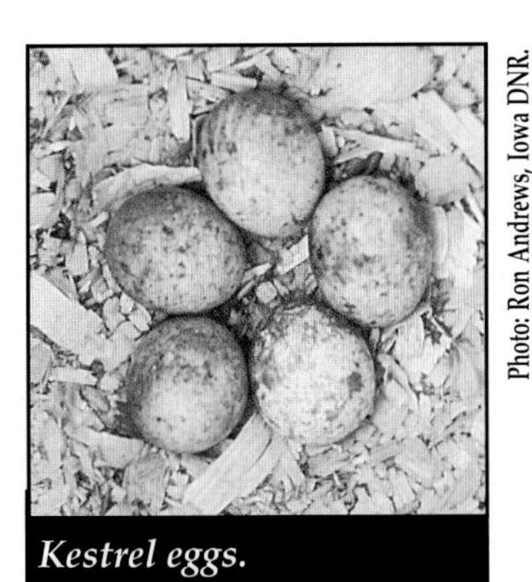

Photo: Ron Andrews, Iowa DNR.

Kestrel eggs.

Photo: Paul Schmitt

A female kestrel broods its young.

The lack of suitable nesting cavities appears to be a significant limiting factor for kestrels. In one study done in Colorado, a local population increased from 6 pairs to at least 25 pairs after nest boxes were provided.

Kestrel boxes should be installed by February 1 to have a good chance of being used in their first year because kestrels are one of the first migrants to return from their wintering grounds.

Starlings may be a persistent problem in a kestrel box. The boxes will need to be checked regularly—every week or 10 days—to remove starling eggs and nests. Starlings are an unprotected species.

Kestrels normally lay five eggs that are white, pinkish-white or cinnamon, and they are evenly covered with small spots of brown. Occasional checking of the nest will not cause the kestrels to abandon the nest.

Adult kestrel, a common farmland raptor.

19. Common Barn Owl

Figures 15 & 16 (Pages 97 & 98)

The "common" barn owl is one of the rarest owls in the Midwest. It was once fairly common in farmland landscape that included meadows, haylands, and pastures. In those habitats the barn owl could seek prey like meadow voles (field mice). If the right habitats are present, they can be surprisingly tolerant of humans. They will nest in barns, silos, granaries, grain elevators, hollow trees, and even church steeples.

The conversion of mixed agricultural landscapes to row crops and a concurrent decline of grassland rodents has caused a dramatic decline in barn owl populations. Another suspected cause of their decline is the increase in numbers of great horned owls. Great horned owls prey on barn owls and are now numerous in many areas formerly occupied by barn owls.

These owls are **very** sensitive to disturbance during April and May. They will abandon a nest if it is disturbed during these months. Barn owl clutches average six eggs and incubation lasts approximately 32 days.

A pair of barn owls may capture up to 1,000 rodents per season to feed themselves and their young. The chicks fly at 8 to 10 weeks of age.

A barn owl nesting box can be placed in a covered silo (Figure 15) or in an abandoned or seldom-used barn (Figure 16). It is best to have some hayfields,

Ron Anderson of the Minnesota Department of Natural Resources displays a completed barn owl nest box ready for placement.

Tim Tuthill of the Minnesota Department of Natural Resources is placing a barn owl nest box at the top of a covered, empty silo.

This barn owl nest box is ready for occupancy.

Barn owl chicks.

The common barn owl is one of our most beautiful owls.

meadows, or "conservation reserve program" set-aside acres near the silo or barn as rodent-hunting habitat.

For a silo-mounted nest box, securely knot one end of the mounting rope cord and thread it through the end furthest from the entry hole so that the knot is inside the box. Pull the box up inside the silo. Loop the free end of the rope twice around the door frame at the top of the silo so that the box hangs near the top of the inside of the silo. The entry hole faces to the center of the silo. Obviously, the silo must have a roof, but there must be an opening for the owls to enter. While positioning the nest box it is handy to hold the box in place with a bungie cord. Then thread the rope through the remaining rope hole, reach into the box, and knot the rope inside. Adjust the box so it hangs level.

The other alternative for barn owl nest box placement is to place the box on a cross-beam in the hayloft area on the inside of the barn. It is best to place the box on the end of the barn. The box should be 20 to 25 feet above the ground.

The open-fronted box should be placed against the inside of the barn wall after cutting a 6"x6" entrance hole in the barn wall approximately 7inches above the beam. This height is important to keep the young owls from falling out of the box. Position the box so the entrance is approximately 2 inches from one end and nail it through the bottom of the box to the cross beam. If the beam is narrow, provide additional board supports under the box or use supplemental ropes or wires to secure the box to the wall.

Barn owl pellets should be cleaned out of nest boxes at the end of the nesting season. You may wish to donate these pellets to a local science teacher so they can do a class project on barn owl food habits.

The nest box design shown here was developed by the Ohio Department of Natural Resources. The recommendations on placement and nest box management are based on recommendations by barn owl experts Bruce A. Colvin and Paul Hegdal.

Part 2

Nest boxes and platforms for use in extensive stands of deciduous or coniferous forest

Photo: Steve Wilson

Young boreal owl.

Photo: Fred K. Truslow

Adult barred owl.

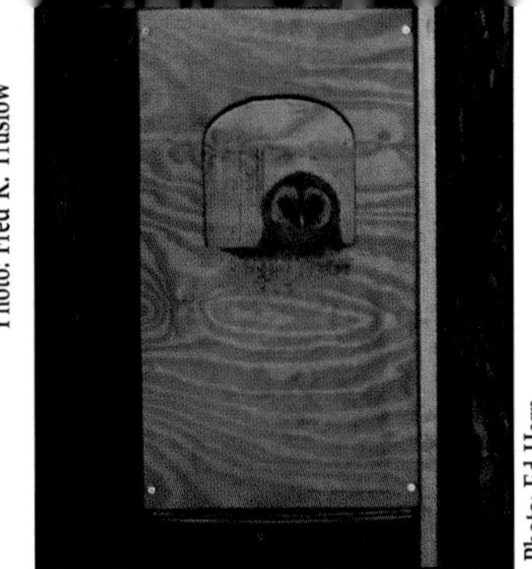

Hello, world!

Photo: Ed Harp

Photo: Ed Harp

Barred owl chicks.

Barred owl nest boxes can be checked through the entrance ho

20. Barred Owl

Figure 12 (page 94)

The barred owl is one of our more common owls in hardwood forests. Its call is a distinctive "Who-cooks-for-you." Its brown eyes with blue pupils are unique. The barred owl nest box is made of 3/4-inch-thick exterior grade plywood. Do not paint, stain, or treat the box with creosote. Put a 2- to 3-inch-layer of small wood chips in the bottom of the box. No cleaning is needed except to remove leaves and other litter that squirrels put into the box. The entrance hole is 7 inches wide and 7 inches high with a rounded top and rounded corners at the bottom. The hole can be either on the front or on a side, but if it is on the side, the box is easier to clean. This box can be cleaned out through the hole, so the roof does not need to be hinged.

The barred owl nest box as shown in Figure 12 may be usurped by squirrels. If you have a problem with squirrels, try removing the roof of the barred owl nest box. Squirrels are less prone to use a topless nest box.

Another effective design for barred owls is to use the common merganser pattern in Figure 18 with some modifications: The front and sides should be 18inches long. The back should be 26 inches long, not 32 inches. The roof should be left out, and no entrance hole is necessary because the top is left open.

Barred owl boxes must be spaced a half mile from each other because these owls defend a territory of 400 to 600 acres per pair.

The box should be cleaned out or placed in January. The box should be located 20 to 30 feet high in a mature upland hardwood or lowland hardwood area, and preferably within 200 feet of water. Do not place the box on the edge of a clearing or within 150 feet of a residence. The entrance hole should not be obscured by branches or leaves, but a perch should be near enough to the box so that the young can "branch" out onto it as they leave the nest. The box should be placed on a living hardwood tree or a conifer with a relatively open, exposed trunk.

Ensuring an open flight path to the nest box is highly desirable. Owls typically have a low level flight path with an upward swing to the box entrance or nearby branch. Removal of a few small trees in front of the box may allow easier access.

Placement of boxes can help prevent predation. Don't place boxes near major game trails. Raccoon predation can also be reduced by placing a 2-foot-wide sheet of tin or aluminum around the tree at chest height.

This design has been developed by David H. (DJ) Johnson, Rural Route 6, Box 410, Mankato, MN 56001. If you try a barred owl nest box, let him know your results.

.1. Great Crested Flycatcher

'igure 5 (page 86

This fascinating songbird of our ıardwood forests, orchards, and ›arks is grayish above with a yel-ɔwish breast. It is more often heard han seen. The call is an ascending ɔud whistle "Wheeeep!" The nests re often characterized by the pres-ınce of shed snake skins that have ›een placed there by the flycatch-ırs. The bulky nest also includes wigs, leaves, hair, feathers and ›ark fibers.

Great crested flycatchers will ıse the one-board bluebird house n Figure 5, except that the en-rance hole should be 1 3/4 inches in diameter. Chances of use are best if the house is placed from 10 to 20 feet high. Doug Keran of Brainerd reports that flycatchers tend to use nest boxes in pine trees, in mixed conifer, and hardwood stands.

Nest boxes should be placed in woodlands and woodland edges. Both sparrow **and** starling control may be necessary.

Newly fledged flycatchers are a real treat to see. They cling to the side of trees like fuzzy little woodpeckers.

Photo: Dick Peterson

Great crested flycatcher.

22. Prothonotary Warbler

Figure 1 (page 80)

The prothonotary warbler was referred to by Dr. Thomas S. Roberts in *Birds of Minnesota* as the "Golden Swamp Warbler." The name is very appropriate. This warbler is orange-yellow with wings and tail that are slate-blue. This beautiful songbird pioneered into southeastern Minnesota from 1870 to 1890, and has now spread northward to Isanti and Washington counties. It is found on bottomland hardwood forests of the Mississippi River from Houston County northward to the Twin Cities, along river valleys like the Root River near Rochester, along the St. Croix River valley in east-central Minnesota, and along the Rum River northward to Isanti County. It usually nests in flooded backwater habitats that are characterized by woodland pools and oxbow ponds. Its nest is typically an abandoned downy woodpecker hole in a dead willow snag in standing water. Often the nest will be no more than 3 to 5 feet above the water level.

Most people don't realize that this beautiful woodland warbler is rather adaptable and will use birdhouses.

If you live near lowland hardwood forest habitat within the range of this warbler, try using the birdhouse plan in Figure 1. Use a 1 1/4-inch diameter hole. Place the house on a snag or post in shallow woodland pools or in oxbow ponds of river bottom habitat, 3 to 5 feet above the water level. If predator guards are used on free standing posts, nests can also be placed on adjacent shoreline habitat with the hole facing the open water. Prothonotary warblers will also nest in these birdhouses if they are placed on the sides of homes or outbuildings near water.

Photo: D. B. Pettingill/VIREO

Prothonotary warbler.

Photo: John Mathisen

Saw-whet owl chick.

Northern saw-whet owl.

A saw-whet owl peers from a nest box.

23. Northern Saw-whet Owl

Figure 13 (page 95)

The northern saw-whet owl is our smallest owl—only 7 inches high. It does not have ear tufts like the screech-owl. It is seldom seen, but more common than formerly believed.

Preferred habitat includes coniferous or deciduous forest, mixed stands of conifers and hardwoods, woodlots, and swamps. Saw-whet owls will use the same type of nest box as northern screech-owls use.

Saw-whet owl nests are usually quite high—14 feet off the ground or higher. Nest boxes should be placed in live mature trees. Doug Keran in Brainerd has reported the most success with boxes placed in red pine and jack pine trees. Areas near water seem to be preferred. As with screech-owl nests, 2 to 3 inches of wood chips should be placed in the bottom of the box.

The nest box can be checked by gently tapping on the side. The owl will peek out of the entrance hole without leaving the box.

24. Boreal Owl

Figure 13 (page 95)

Several years ago a pair of boreal owls was first recorded nesting in Minnesota. They are more common than formerly believed. Research by Steve Wilson and Bill Lane in Minnesota has revealed that there is a population of these appealing little owls in the northern arrowhead region of Minne-

Photo: Steven Wilson

Boreal owl adult.

sota from northern St. Louis County eastward to northern Lake and Cook counties. More can be learned about the occurrence of this owl by placing nest boxes like the screech-owl design in Figure 13.

Boreal owls usually nest in abandoned woodpecker holes like those of the pileated woodpecker and they have attempted nesting in wood duck boxes in the Superior National Forest. Boreal owls utilize cavities in overmature aspen stands so this might be one type of habitat where nest boxes could be used to enhance a population. They normally nest in aspen trees that are at least 11 inches in diameter.

Boreal owl chick.

The habitat of boreal owls includes overmature mixed coniferous/deciduous forest adjacent to lowland conifer forest. They will also use younger forest stands where there are still a few large diameter aspen or birch for use as nesting trees. These stands of forest are better if there are scattered clumps of taller conifers for song perches. These conifers can include spruce, fir, cedar, white pine, and jack pine but not red pine. Boreal owls do not seem to use monoculture stands of even-age forest.

Photo: Steven Wilson

The best reward for placing nest boxes for wildlife is the satisfaction of helping a species like the boreal owl.

Try placing nest boxes from 16 to 20 feet high in live hardwood trees. Nest boxes should be placed within 100 yards of several tall conifers or a clump of conifers and also near a stand of lowland conifer habitat like a cedar swamp. The front of the box should not be obscured by branches.

Please report any nesting success to Steve Wilson, Deptartment of Natural Resources, 2005 Highway 37, Evelyth, MN 55734.

Northern screech-owl.

25. Northern Screech-Owl

Figure 13 ((page 95

Northern screech-owls are small gray or reddish owls with ear tufts that live in our hardwood forests. They are about 8 inches tall and resemble a miniature version of the more common great horned owl. The nest box for screech-owls shown in Figure 13 should be placed at least 10 feet high in a hardwood forest. Preferred habitat seems to be on the edge of woods adjacent to fields or wetlands. To prevent use by squirrels the box could be placed on a pole with a predator guard. Since the entrance hole is 3 inches in diameter, persistent starling control may be necessary. About 2 to 3 inches of wood chips should be placed in the bottom of the nesting box.

This flying squirrel moved into a wren house after chewing on the entrance to enlarge the hole. It lived in the front yard of a Minneapolis home in 1991.

Photo: Dominique Braud

ech-owl on nest.

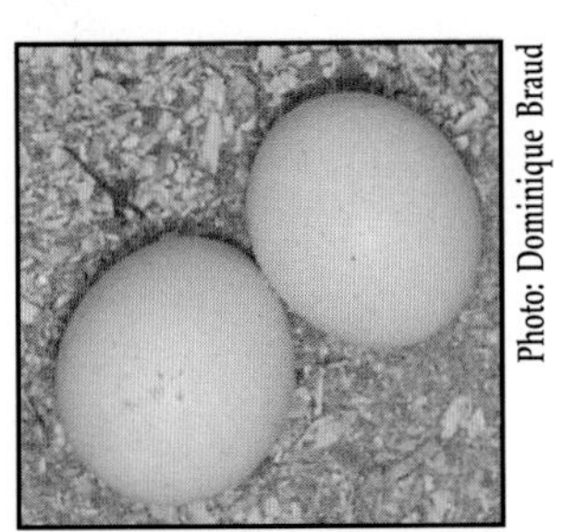

Photo: Dominique Braud

Screech-owl eggs.

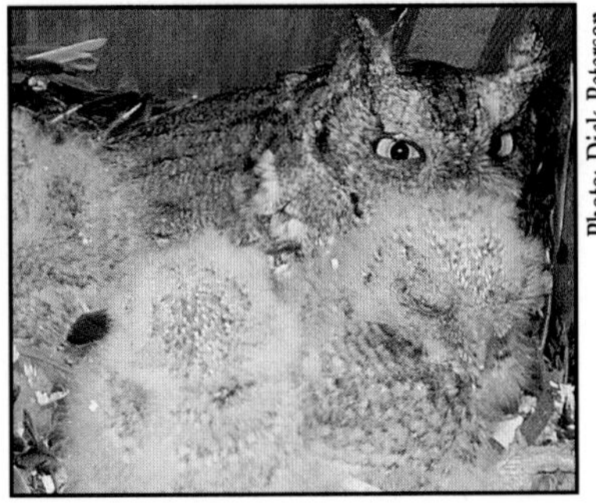

Photo: Dick Peterson

Adult screech-owl with young.

Photo: Dick Peterson

These young screech owls were raised in a nest box in Minneapolis in 1990.

26. Northern and Southern Flying Squirrel

Figure 1 (page 80)

The spritely flying squirrel is nocturnal and is seldom ever seen, even where it is common. It may come out at night to feed in backyard bird feeders. Flying squirrels are found in a wide variety of habitats ranging from northern coniferous forests to groves and woodlots in southern Minnesota. It is probably not necessary to put out nest boxes specifically for flying squirrels because they readily use boxes that are put out for other species, including wood duck and screech-owl boxes. The house wren box in Figure 1 is an especially good size for flying squirrels but the entrance hole should be 1 1/4 inch in diameter. Nest boxes should be placed in heavily wooded sites to help avert competition from house sparrows.

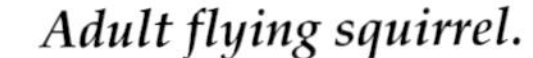

Adult flying squirrel.

27. Great Horned Owl

Figure 14 (page 96)

The great horned owl is one of Minnesota's most common owls. It is found in an incredible variety of habitats ranging from farm woodlots and shelterbelts to large stands of hardwood forest. Since owls do not construct their own nests, they will readily adapt to nesting cones that are placed in suitable habitat.

The great horned owl nesting cone is made by using a 3' x 3' piece of 1 inch mesh chicken wire. The chicken wire is made into a shallow cone by cutting from one corner to the center and then overlapping the two cut edges until the cone is about 18 inches deep. The cut ends of the chicken wire are then bent around the overlapping wire. The cone is then lined with tar paper, and provided with a drainage hole at the base. Nest material is then added to the cone and consists of twigs, leaves, and branches, with finer material near the top. Larger branches are interwoven with each other and the chicken wire as tightly as possible. Flexible shrubs like willow and dogwood are excellent for weaving around the top edge of the nest so that a solid interwoven nest structure is created—not just a pile of sticks. The completed nest is then tied to a rope, pulled up the tree, and secured in a suitable crotch with wire and/or large staples. Nests should be put out in the fall if they are to be located and used by great horned owls the following January.

In central Minnesota, great horned owls usually nest in red-tailed hawk nests that are about 45 feet high. Great horned owls will

Photo: Katherine Haws

Owl nest platform.

Photo: Carol Dorff

Great horned owl at its nest.

This young great horned owl has left its nest and can fly but has not grown its adult plumage yet. It is about eight weeks old.

nest lower, however, and would likely accept nest platforms that are 15 to 20 feet high. The nest platform should be placed in a live hardwood tree that is at least 12 inches in diameter. Good sites would be remote corners of farm groves, or large trees in shelterbelts and farm windbreaks. A key feature to look for is a crotch that would facilitate placement of the platform.

One reason that people may wish to attract great horned owls to their property is to help remove cottontail rabbits in orchards or farm groves where shrubs are being damaged by the rabbits. Great horned owls are also one of the only predators that regularly eat skunks. This is particularly important in Minnesota where skunks are the main carrier of rabies.

The nest design is provided by Bob Bohm from the following article: Bohm, R.T., 1977. "Artificial Nest Platforms for Raptors". *Raptor Research* 11(4):97-99.

28. Eastern Red Squirrel

Figure 13 (page 95)

The eastern red squirrel, like the flying squirrel, is adaptable to a wide variety of habitats ranging from northern coniferous forests to farm woodlots in southern Minnesota. The screech-owl box in Figure 13 is appropriate for use by eastern red squirrels, and they will also use wood duck boxes. They are extremely aggressive at bird feeders and regularly eat the eggs and young of songbirds. For these reasons, they are not among the more favored tenants of nest boxes.

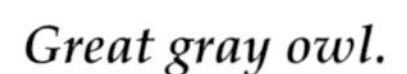

Great gray owl.

29. Great Gray Owl

Figure 14 (page 96)

Few people would guess that the magnificent great gray owl regularly nests in Minnesota and is readily attracted to nesting platforms. Like great horned owls, they do not construct their own nests. They will usually nest in abandoned raven, red-tailed hawk, or goshawk nests.

There are two primary areas of great gray owl habitat in Minnesota. The Roseau Bog in Roseau County is famous for its high concentration of great gray owls and the long-term studies done by Dr. Robert Nero from Winnipeg, Canada. Ideal habitat for great gray owls is tamarack lowlands where the trees are at least 5 inches in diameter and about 15 percent of the habitat is in openings. The owls feed on small mammals, including mice, lemmings, and voles. Nests are most easily secured in the tops or crotches of deformed tamarack trees. They should be placed 15 to 20 feet high.

Nest structures have also been successfully used in northeastern Minnesota including Aitkin, Pine, Carlton, and St. Louis counties. They may be placed in lowland hardwoods, tamarack stands, or even upland maple-basswood forest. Forest lands in the region around Palisade, Minn., and the lowlands west of Floodwood, Minn., are particularly good areas for great gray owls.

The nest structure shown in Figure 14 should be placed in the interior of forest stands, not on the edge. Snags in the vicinity of openings are useful as sites from which prey can be hunted.

Recommendations for great gray owl nest platforms have been derived from information provided by Dr. Robert Nero of Winnipeg, Canada, and Steve Loch of Foley, Minn.

30. Pileated Woodpecker

Figure 17 (page 99)

The distinctive pileated woodpecker occurs throughout much of the hardwood forest zone of southeastern, east-central and central Minnesota. It is the largest woodpecker in the state—about the size of a crow.

It has not been known to nest in nesting boxes because it is a primary excavator and must excavate its own nesting cavity. However, the breakthrough in attracting flickers developed by Mr. A.J. Boersma of Sioux City, Iowa, may apply to pileated woodpeckers also. The trick is to fill the nest box with sawdust all the way to the top and tamp it in. Then the woodpecker can fulfill its instinct to make its own nest cavity.

Photo: Dick Peterson

Young pileated woodpeckers beg for food.

This nest box design is proposed as an experiment for woodland owners, naturalists, and biologists to try. Use the design shown in Figure 17, but use 1 1/2-inch-thick cedar instead of 3/4-inch-thick board as called for in the plan. Also, a 12-foot-long, 2" x 12" board will be necessary to make this box. The floor section must be 8 1/4 inches long instead of 9 3/4 inches as shown in Figure 17.

The entrance hole should be 4 inches in diameter and centered 19 inches above the floor. The top should be hinged to allow filling with sawdust. The entrance should probably face south or east. Sawdust should be tamped into the box all the way to the top.

The box should be placed about 20 to 30 feet high in a live or dead hardwood tree in the interior of a stand of mature hardwoods where pileated woodpeckers are known to occur. If a live tree is used, lag bolts and washers can be used to attach the house to the tree so it can be loosened as the tree grows. Caution: Dead trees are often unsafe to climb and may frequently be undesirable to use for that reason. Please report any nest box use by pileated woodpeckers to the Nongame Wildlife Program.

Photo: Dick Peterson

Pileated woodpecker.

Adult bald eagle.

31. Bald Eagle

No Figure

Wildlife managers have had limited success attracting bald eagles to artificial nest platforms. They normally will nest in the crotch of a tall white pine tree in coniferous forests. Farther south, they will use other tall species like cottonwood trees.

John Olson, a DNR wildlife manager from Wisconsin, has found that the most effective technique for placing a bald eagle nest platform is to cut off the top of a tall tree where it is 4 to 5 inches in diameter. This will not kill the tree. The nest platform is placed on top. If this is done on a white pine, in 4 to 5 years the lateral branches will grow up and arch over the nest to create a natural shading effect. Bald eagles seem to prefer a nest with some shade.

F.L. Johnson and Ron Eckstein have developed a pattern for a bald eagle nest platform that can be placed either on a tree top or on the side of a tree. These platforms would only need to be used in unusual circumstances because suitable nesting sites do not appear to be a limiting factor for bald eagles in most of Minnesota.

Minnesota Department of Natural Resources wildlife biologist Steve Kittelson displays a newly constructed bald eagle platform.

Part 3

Nest boxes and platforms for use in lakes, rivers, marshes, ponds, and adjacent upland habitats

Craig Henderson checks a wood duck box near Hugo, Minn. Building and placing wood duck nest boxes has helped the wood duck make a dramatic recovery.

Photo: Dr. Scott Nielsen

A hen w duck accomp newly hatche duckli a sprin marsh.

32. Wood Duck

Figure 18 (page 100)

The wood duck box has helped the beautiful wood duck make a remarkable recovery during the past 30 years. Early in this century some people believed the wood duck was becoming extinct. Now it is one of Minnesota's most abundant waterfowl species.

The entrance hole should be an oval 3 inches high and 4 inches wide, as shown in Figure 27 . This hole excludes most raccoons. The hole should be centered 19.5 inches above the base. A 15" x 3" strip of 1/4-inch mesh hardware cloth should be cut out and the cut edges folded back. This should be attached inside the box under the entrance to function as a ladder for the newly hatched ducklings. Sometimes squirrels will tear this ladder loose so it will need to be checked annually. Or the wood under the entrance hole should be roughened with a chisel to give the ducklings the toe-holds they need. The roughened area should extend below the entrance hole for 1 foot. At least 4 inches of cedar shavings should be placed in the nest to serve as nesting material.

The house should be constructed of wood that is strong and can be made weather resistant. It can be painted, stained, or treated on the outside only. The floor should be recessed 1/4 inch up from the lower edge of the sides to prevent rotting.

Houses can be placed on an isolated tree or on a 16-foot-long, 4"x4" post that is cypress, cedar, or preservative-treated wood. An aluminum or tin sheet should be nailed around the post under the house to prevent squirrels and raccoons from climbing. Since wood ducks are not territorial, two or more houses can be placed on the same post or tree.

New information by Dr. Paul Sherman and Brad Semel at Cornell University has revealed that high densities of conspicuous wood duck nest boxes contribute to a high rate of "dump nesting." This occurs when many hens lay up to 30 or 40 eggs in a single nest box. This behavior is counter productive. It is better to scatter nest boxes in woodland and wetland habitats so that each box is visibly isolated from other wood duck nest boxes and is relatively inconspicuous.

Vigilant starling control will be necessary in wood duck boxes. Remove their nests and eggs whenever they occur. The top of a wood duck box should be fastened to its support so that it leans forward a couple inches. This facilitates the drainage of rainwater. This also makes it easier for the newly hatched ducklings to climb up the front of the box when they are ready to jump to the ground.

Boxes placed on posts in water should be at least 3 feet above the high water mark. Wood duck boxes should be placed over water or in woodland habitat up to half-a-mile from lakes, ponds, marshes, and rivers. Since the hen must lead her ducklings to water after they hatch, the habitat between the house location and the water's edge should be free of major obstacles like highways, fences with small mesh wire, and street curbing.

Heights above 20 feet seem to be preferred in trees. Aspen trees should be avoided. They are vulnerable to being cut by beavers. Box entrances near water should face the water. Otherwise, there seems to be a slight preference for south and west facing entrance holes. Ideally, boxes on land should be 30 to 100 feet from the water's edge—not at the water's edge. Boxes at the water's edge are more vulnerable to predation by raccoons.

Annual maintenance on wood duck boxes should be completed by March 1. Boxes should be opened, inspected, and more wood shavings added if necessary.

When you check wood duck boxes in the spring, be adequately prepared. You will need a wrench for loosening the lag bolts, a hammer, extra roofs, at least one sack of wood shavings, nails, rope, wire, and an extension ladder. Take along a caulking gun to caulk cracks or joints that have loosened up on the house. This will help keep the house waterproof.

The design shown in Figure 18 is different from the first version of Woodworking for Wildlife. This design has been developed by Don "The Duckman" Helmeke of Minneapolis, J.W. Busch of North Carolina, and Glenn Meyer, the editor of Outdoor News. This new design is an improvement on past designs because it is lighter, easier to clean and check, and more weatherproof.

Weatherproofing

This box is more weatherproof because it uses cedar boards with the rough side out, the roof overlaps the front and back, the roof slopes to shed rain, and the floor is recessed upward one-half inch.

Nails (Screws)

Cedar boards can split easily when being nailed, so it is best to drill nail holes with a bit slightly smaller than the diameter of the nails used. Smooth galvanized nails "loosen up" too easily. Use sheet rock screws and a screw-gun to assemble the house. Thin "grip" or "anchor" type cedar shake nails 2 1/2 inches long will also work, except where the horizontal cleat spacer is nailed to the rear wall. Use a 1 1/2 inch nail there.

Cleaning

Top-opening nest boxes are more difficult to clean than side opening boxes. This design uses two nails as the pivot points for the side door. It is much easier to check the nest and add wood shavings with this design.

Size

Traditional wood duck nest box designs have used 12-inch wide lumber—resulting in quite heavy nest boxes. This box is lighter to carry and raise into a tree. Wood ducks, goldeneyes, and hooded mergansers have all used this size box successfully.

Mounting the Box

The easiest way to mount a wood duck box is to use an aluminum extension ladder to reach a suitable height on a tree or pole. Place a large washer onto a 5/16" x 4-1/2" lag bolt. Use a hammer to start the lag bolt into the tree or pole, then use a wrench to begin twisting it in until about 2-1/2 inches are still exposed.

There should be a 3/4 inch diameter hole in the back of the wood duck box straight back from the entrance hole.

Pull the wood duck box up from the ground with a rope and set the house onto the lag bolt through the 3/4 inch bolt hole. Set a Duckman "speed mount" washer onto the lag bolt inside the box, and tighten the bolt. (Be sure the top of the house leans slightly forward to help the ducklings

Craig Henderson (left) and Jeff Stedman (right) built this wood duck nest box as part of a 4-H wildlife project. Art Hawkins of Hugo, Minn., helped them place the box in good habitat. Within one week after placing the box, it was occupied by a hen "woodie."

climb their ladder after hatching.) Then use a lag bolt and washer to fasten in the hole at the bottom of the box. The lag bolt will need to be loosened every spring to allow for tree growth. Complete hardware kits, including speed mounting washers, lag bolts, nails, and turn buttons are available from Don "The Duckman" Helmeke at 15702—105th Avenue N., Maple Grove, MN 55369. He also has a flexible fiberglass wrap that can be wrapped around trees to keep raccoons from climbing trees. Contact Don for current prices of the wood duck hardware kits and fiberglass wrap.

One other very popular type of wood duck box is the plastic "Tom Tubbs" box that is sold by the Robbinsdale Farm and Garden Store, 4125 Richard Ave. N., Robbinsdale, MN 55422 (612-533-2244), or The Bird House, 5898 Omaha Ave. N., Stillwater, MN 55082 (612-439-1923). This box should be used in shaded sites only.

Recommendations for wood duck box construction and maintenance have been contributed primarily by DNR waterfowl biologist Mike Zicus, Art Hawkins, Don "Duckman" Helmeke, and Lyle Bradley from Anoka County.

If you wish to learn more about attracting wood ducks with nest boxes, you can subscribe to the "Wood Duck Newsgram" for $5.00 per year. Requests should be sent to Lloyd Knudson, Treasurer, 5463 W. Broadway Avenue, Forest Lake, MN 55025.

Photo: Dick Peterson

A wood duck nes is lined with down and may contain twelve o more eggs.

Photo: Dr. Scott Nielsen

Hen and drake wood duck.

Photo: Dick Peterson

A hen wood duck incubating its eggs.

Photo: Dick Peterson

The eggs hatch after an incubation period of about 30 days.

Photo: Dominique Braud/Don Enger

Wood ducks normally leave their nest box in the morning on the day after they hatch.

Photo: Ray Cunningham

Adult hen common merganser.

Photo: Ray Cunningham

The hen common merganser is an unusual but welcome occupant of nest boxes.

33. Common Merganser

Figure 17 (page 99)

Few people realize that the common merganser sometimes nests in tree cavities. They are found in northeastern Minnesota including the counties of Cook, Lake, St. Louis, Itasca, and surrounding area. Mr. Ray Cunningham of Floodwood, Minn. and area wildlife manager Jim Schneeweis of Grand Rapids, have discovered that they will use nest boxes. Mr. Cunningham has been successfully raising common mergansers along the St. Louis River since 1979.

Mr. Cunningham has placed such boxes 12 to 17 feet high in trees on land immediately adjacent to water and on flooded dead elm trees 8 feet high over water. The boxes should be placed with the entrance clear of obstructions and facing adjacent rivers and ponds. The entrance hole should be an oval 5 inches high and 6 inches wide. The entrance hole is large enough that the box can be cleaned out through the hole. A hinged roof is not necessary.

Place a horizontal piece of slab wood with the bark attached immediately below the entrance hole on the front of the box. It will aid the hen in landing and entering the hole.

These boxes are vulnerable to raccoon predation. If raccoons prove to be a problem, these nest boxes should be placed on predator proof posts.

Mergansers fly in low and swoop upward to enter the nest box, so the boxes need to be at least 8 to10 feet above ground, or if over water, should be at least 3 feet above the high water mark.

34. Hooded Merganser

Figure 18 (page 100)

The beautiful hooded merganser nests primarily in the forests of north central Minnesota in habitat adjacent to lakes, beaver ponds, swamps, and rivers. It also nests sporadically across southern Minnesota. It nests in the same type of nest box that wood ducks use. The desired entry hole is the same size, and all nest box management considerations are the same as for the wood duck. Boxes should be placed at least 8to10 feet above ground, or if over water, they should be at least 3 feet above the high water mark. They seem to prefer west-facing entrance holes.

Photo: Dr. Scott Nielsen

Drake hooded merganser.

Photo: Ray Cunningham

This hen common merganser was incubating its eggs near Floodwood, Minnesota.

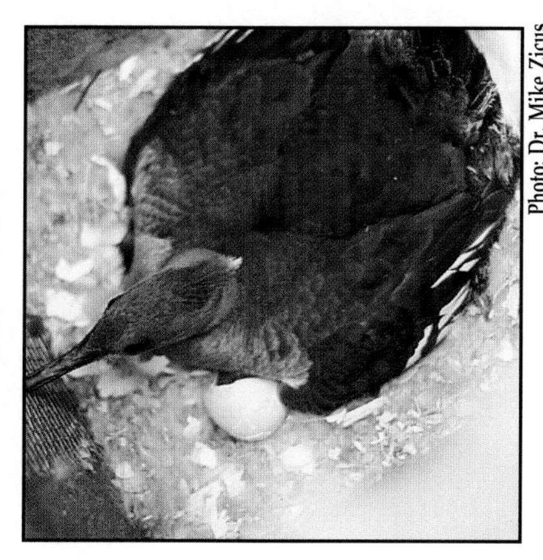

Photo: Dr. Mike Zicus

The incubation period for hooded merganser eggs is about 32-33 days.

35. Common Goldeneye

Figure 18 (page 100)

If duck boxes of the style shown in Figure 18 are to be placed in northern Minnesota (including Cass, Beltrami, Koochiching, Itasca, Lake of the Woods, St. Louis, Lake and Cook counties) it is desirable to use an oval entrance hole that is 3 1/4 inches high and 4 1/4 inches wide. This size hole will allow the common goldeneye to nest in the box as well as the wood duck and hooded merganser. A hen goldeneye is shown on page 15.

Notice that this hole size is slightly smaller than previously recommended. Goldeneyes seem to have no problem using this smaller size, and it gives better protection from entry by raccoons.

Common loon eggs hatch after about 29 days.

Photo: James LaVigne

Male and female loons take turns incubating the eggs.

36. Common Loon

Figure 19 (page 102)

The common loon, Minnesota's state bird, usually nests on islands or on shorelines of our northern lakes. On some lakes or reservoirs, loons experience frequent nest failures because of water level fluctuations or because their mainland nesting sites are vulnerable to predation by raccoons or other predators.

In such cases, a floating nesting platform can provide a more secure site for loons to nest on. Because of the high degree of development on many lakes in northeastern states like New Hampshire, such platforms now provide a substantial portion of the loon production in that region.

It is important to place the nest platform in a location that is reasonably sheltered from wind action. In most cases this means anchoring it within 30 to 50 feet of the shoreline on the west or northwest side of a lake. Wind-sheltered bays that are connected to larger lakes are ideal. Figure A, page 67, shows some examples of where to locate a loon nesting platform.

Important! Loon nesting platforms can be a hazard to boaters. To avoid safety hazards and legal liability in Minnesota, place reflectors on all four sides of the nest platform and register the nest platform with the county sheriff in the same manner that you would register a swimming raft.

Supplies needed to make a loon nesting platform are five dried ce-

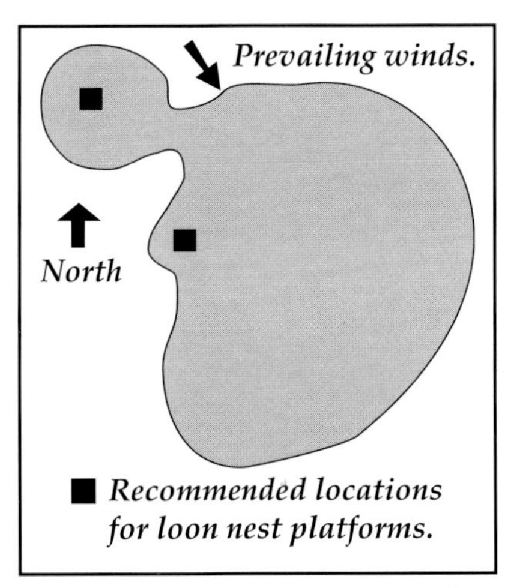

Figure A

dar posts, 6 feet long and 10 inches in diameter; a 6' x 6' section of 12 1/2 gauge 2" x 4" zinc-coated welded wire; 1 1/2 pounds of 1 1/2 inch fence staples; 24— No. 60 spikes for fastening the cedar frame at the notches; 30 feet of No. 9 wire for lashing the frame; four cable clamps to secure rope or cable to 3/16- inch wire cable for anchor raft and anchor blocks; 30 feet of lines; two 8" x 8" x 16" concrete blocks or equivalent for anchors; boughs, cattails, rushes, moss, sedge mat, or equivalent to cover the platform to make it look natural; and two bushels of old reeds for nest building to be added immediately after ice-out in the spring.

To build the loon nesting platform, notch, spike, and wire the framework of the platform. Staple welded wire onto the bottom of the three parallel logs by placing staples 4 inches apart with double rows of staples on each log. Attach anchor lines at two opposite corners. Fill the raft with cattails, rushes (roots and all) and sedge mat. The water should be at least 2 to 3 feet deep. There should be at least 3 feet of slack in the anchor lines to allow for high water. To help prevent this platform from eventually becoming waterlogged and sinking, it may be desirable to fasten a several-inch layer of styrofoam on top of the wire screen before adding the marsh vegetation.

This information has been provided by Mr. John Mathisen, Forest Biologist, Chippewa National Forest, Cass Lake, Minn.

Photo: Cornell Lab of Ornithology

Constructing a loon nest platform can be a good project for a lake association.

Photo: Cornell Lab of Ornithology

Some aquatic vegetation is planted on the loon nesting platform so it looks like a small floating island.

This loon was using a nest platform near Nisswa, Minn.

37. Double-crested Cormorant

Figure 20 (page 103)

The double-crested cormorant is a black waterbird about the size of a goose. It has been increasing in numbers throughout the Great Lakes States. Cormorants readily use nest platforms like those explained for the great blue heron. They may nest in colonies with great-blue herons or they may occur in colonies comprised of cormorants only. As with great blue herons, nest platforms should be placed in or adjacent to existing colonies.

Western painted turtles will readily use floating logs or platforms that c

Photo: Wisconson DNR

Heron nest platform under construction.

Photo: Katherine Haws

Heron nest platform in use.

38. Great Blue Heron

Figure 20 (page 103)

The great blue heron is one of Minnesota's most conspicuous waterbirds. Great blue herons are found across most of the state. A colonial-nesting species, they typically nest in live or dead trees that are on islands, peninsulas, or shoreline woods. Usually the best management for their colonies is to protect the colony from disturbance during the nesting season.

In some cases, herons will nest in dead trees in newly created reservoirs or in beaver ponds. These trees can be expected to deteriorate and fall within five to 15 years of flooding. When this occurs on public land, it may be advisable to try to retain the colony on the site where it can be adequately protected, managed, viewed by the public. Sometimes colonies on private land are more vulnerable to harassment, shooting by vandals, or untimely woodcutting activities that can jeopardize the heron's nesting success.

Colonies in dead trees can be preserved in those locations by providing nest platforms on cedar power poles. Platforms constructed on new poles have a 45-year life expectancy.

The support poles should be 30-foot cedar power poles that are at least 8 to 10 inches in diameter at the base. These poles can be obtained new or used from local utility companies.

Three nest platforms can be placed on each pole. Platforms should be spaced 4 feet apart and staggered at 180 degree intervals. The top platform is placed at the top of the pole. Each platform is constructed as shown in Figure 20. Materials are pre-cut, bolt holes drilled, and platforms semi-constructed before going into the field. This includes joining the top and bottom braces for each sidearm with matching bolts. The outer-

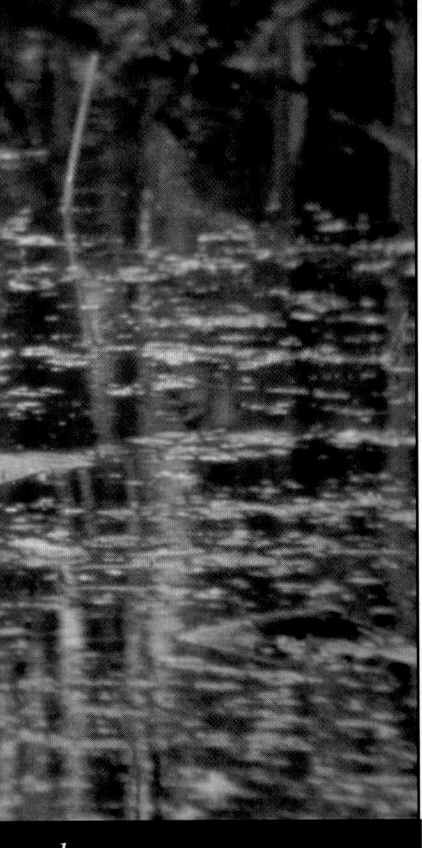
Photo: Earl Kopischke

ponds.

39. Turtle and Duck Loafing Platform

Figure 22 (page 105)

The type of platform described for Canada geese, minus the nesting tub, will work very well along sheltered lakeshores and small ponds as loafing and sunning sites for western painted turtles, wood ducks, mallards, and blue-winged teal. The sites are important because they are relatively safe from predators. Strategically placed platforms can provide enjoyable viewing opportunities for people in front of their lakeshore homes or at wetlands in parks and nature centers. As with loon nesting platforms, this platform when used in Minnesota can be a boating hazard and should have a reflector on each side and be registered with the county sheriff's office.

Photo: Gregory K. Scott

Wood ducks also use floating logs and platforms for loafing and preening.

most nest support on the platform is attached to the sidearms with a 1 foot 9 inch distance between nailing points. This sets the width of the platform. Final construction is done on the ice at the site where the poles are to be erected. As an added inducement for the birds, a small armful of branches could be wired on top of the platform to provide a more secure foundation for the heron's nest.

Soil quality and water depth determine the site to be used. Pole placement should occur in a firm substrate. A clay substrate to a depth of 6 1/2 feet is acceptable. Water depth should be no more than 4 1/2 feet. Sites should be in or adjacent to an existing colony.

The best time to place heronry poles is from January through March. To install a pole, cut a 2' x 2' hole in the ice with a chain saw. A hole is then drilled into the soil under the ice with a hydraulic 8-inch auger mounted on the back of a utility company line truck. A 30-foot post requires a 6-foot deep post hole. If a utility company auger truck can be contracted to do this work, they will have the hydraulic equipment necessary to raise the pole into the ice hole with the platforms attached.

Sidearms are attached to the poles with lag bolts. The lag bolts are driven into the posts with a hammer. The nest platforms are set at approximately 7 degrees above horizontal to provide a pocket for nesting.

To maintain a colony of herons it is desirable to place at least 20 poles. At three nests per pole, this is enough to maintain a colony of up to 60 pairs of birds.

The design for this nest platform has been derived from Katherine Haws, DNR Regional Nongame Specialist, Bemidji, and from T.I. Meier, 1981. *Artificial Nesting Structures for the Double-Crested Cormorant*. Technical Bulletin 126, DNR, Madison, Wis., 12pp.

Photo: Katherine Haws

Examples of properly installed great blue heron nest platforms.

Photo: Dominique Braud

This pair of ospreys has accepted a platform as their nesting site.

40. Osprey

Figure 21 (page 104)

The osprey, or fish hawk, is typically thought of as a wilderness species in northern Minnesota, but it can become adapted to human presence and the use of nesting platforms. People living in beachfront homes on the East Coast once placed old wooden wagon wheels horizontally on poles in their yards to provide nesting sites for ospreys. Farmers considered it good luck to have an osprey nesting at their farmsite.

Photo: Dominique Braud

After mating, the female osprey lays 2 to 4 eggs. They hatch after about 32 days.

Ospreys have been steadily increasing during the past 30 years. Previously they had declined because of the use of DDT pesticide. Ospreys nest on power line transmission towers or in the tops of dead trees in beaver ponds, lakes, and reservoirs. The number of years a given nest may be used is usually limited because the dead trees rot and fall over.

There are some circumstances where it would be advantageous to place a nesting platform for ospreys. If ospreys nest in a hazardous site on a powerline pole, it is possible to place a nesting pole and platform adjacent to the power line. Otherwise move the chicks to the nest platform when they are about four weeks old. The parents should adapt to the new nest, and the old nest can be removed.

Nest platforms and poles can be placed in shallow bogs or wetlands that are frequented by ospreys. Nest platforms can also be put at sites where the existing nest tree has fallen down. Platforms can be placed on old utility poles in open habitats, on "topped" super canopy pines, or on snags adjacent to a shoreline. Developed or intensively used recreation areas should be avoided.

Figure 21 is a diagram of an osprey nest platform. Table 1 is a list of the items needed to construct the platform. A 6 to 8 inch diameter cedar utility pole 20 to 30 feet long is adequate for an osprey nest platform. Poles can be placed in water sites using the techniques explained for the great blue heron nesting poles. Osprey nesting poles on land can be placed by using an auger and by digging a 5-foot deep hole. All nail and bolt holes are pre-drilled to prevent splitting. The wire

Table 1.
Materials needed for Osprey Nest Platform

Two 2" x 6" x 12' cedar boards
One 2" x 6" x 4' cedar board
One 12" x 12" x 1/2" exterior plywood
One 45" x 45" piece of heavy duty wire mesh
Galvanized 40D nails
One 6" or 8" diameter cedar post, 20' to 30' long
Wood preservative and stain

Photo: Steve Kittelson

Photo: Steve Kittelson

Photo: Steve Kittelson

Erecting an osprey nest platform may require assistance from a local utility company. A line truck can help position the nesting pole.

Photo: Dominique Braud

mesh is nailed inside the platform. The whole structure is treated with wood preservative and stained brown. Steel braces are bolted to the platform. Lag bolts are used to secure the platform to the pole or topped pine tree. Some sticks should be wired into the nest to help stimulate use by ospreys.

This information has been derived from F.L. Johnson and V. Wolniewicz, 1979. Platform for Ospreys. Wisconsin DNR Endangered Species Report; and from JoAnn Frier, *Artificial Nesting Structures for Osprey*. New Jersey Division of Fish, Game and Wildlife.

Canada geese usually lay about 5 eggs. The eggs hatch in 26 to 28 days.

41. Canada Goose

Figure 22 (page 105)

The Canada goose has made such a remarkable recovery in Minnesota during the past 30 years that little needs to be done to help ensure their nesting success. There may be local situations, however, where a landowner wishes to enjoy the presence of nesting geese on a particular wetland, or where fluctuating water levels in reservoirs may jeopardize goose nests on muskrat houses or other natural sites. In such cases, a floating nest platform can be a useful alternative as shown in Figure 22.

To make this platform, cut three lengths of 8-inch-diameter cedar power poles 4 feet long. Lay the posts parallel in order to make a 4' x 4' platform on top of the posts. Nail 4-foot lengths of 2" x 6" boards perpendicular to the direction of the posts. Space the boards about 1 inch apart.

Next you will need a galvanized round metal washtub that is 22 inches in diameter and 10 1/2 inches high. These can be purchased at hardware or farm supply stores. One place they can be obtained is from a washtub manufacturer called Behren's, 471 West Third Street, Winona, MN 55987. A low budget alternative to using a washtub is to wire an old tire to the platform and fill it half full of sawdust after covering the slats in the platform beneath it. Sheets of styrofoam fitted under the platform will help keep it from sinking after it eventually becomes waterlogged.

Canada geese begin incubation in early April in Minnesota.

DNR File Photo

Punch about 10 drain holes in the bottom of the washtub. Just under the rolled upper edge of the washtub, cut an escape hatch 6 inches wide and 4 inches high. This is to prevent newly hatched goslings from becoming trapped inside the washtub.

Paint the washtub an earth tone. Nail it onto the center of the platform and fill it one-third full with sawdust.

This platform can be skidded out onto the ice with a snowmobile or towed out with a boat, depending on the time of year. Platforms should be in place by March 15. The best locations are in relatively sheltered areas or bays of marshes. The platforms should be at least 200 yards apart if they are in view of each other to minimize territorial conflicts between nesting pairs. Nest platforms can be closer together if there are trees, peninsulas or other visual barriers between the platform sites. In relatively open water areas, it is best to have the platforms within 20 to 30 feet of shore.

The platform should be placed in 2 to 4 feet of water. A length of welded link chain should be bolted around the cedar posts on opposing corners of the platform. Each chain should be 3 feet longer than the distance from the high water mark to the bottom. Each chain should be bolted to an 8" x 8" x 16" concrete foundation block. The double anchor blocks are dropped about 6 feet apart to prevent the platform from pivoting with the wind.

By mid-March, an armful of grass or wild hay should be placed in the nesting tub to provide nesting material. Most goose nesting will occur from early April through mid-May. Floating goose nest platforms of polyethlene are also available from: Dakota Nesting Structures, 4371 Woodland Park, Valley City, ND 58072. (701) 845-5457, or B & K Fiberglass Rt. 2, Box 28 Garretson, SD 57030 (605) 594-6630

Giant Canada geese readily adapt to the use of nest platforms.

42. Black Tern

No Figure

The black tern is an elegant waterbird that nests in shallow wetlands and marshes of the Midwest. The nests are frequently located on muskrat houses or floating piles of aquatic vegetation. Nests are usually in openings that occur in stands of emergent aquatic plants like giant burreed, narrowleaf cattail, and bulrush. Favored nesting sites are frequently at the tips of peninsulas where stands of emergent vegetation extend into open water.

In some places, fluctuating water levels create problems for success of black tern nests. Dr. Ray Faber of St. Mary's College in Winona, Minn., has developed a nest for black terns. The use of nest platforms may become an important management technique for black terns because this species has declined at a rate of more than 6 percent per year during the past 20 years according to the U.S. Fish and Wildlife Service.

In 1990 in the Trempeleau National Wildlife Refuge in Wisconsin, Dr. Faber documented nest efforts on 7 of 10 available nest platforms. In a total of 10 nest attempts on nest platforms, 8 resulted in successful hatching. On natural sites, only 36 of 78 sites resulted in successful hatching.

The platform is made by using 4 pieces of 32 inch long 2" x 2" pine boards fastened to create a square frame. Chicken wire (one-inch mesh) is stapled onto the top of the square frame.

The platforms are placed singly in openings amid emergent vegetation in mid-May where nesting has been observed in previous years. Each platform is held in place by tying an 8 foot length of light nylon cord from the frame to a wooden stake that is pushed into the marsh bottom. Submerged aquatic vegetation is gathered and piled onto the chicken wire to create a small gradually sloping mound in the center of the frame. Vegetation is added until the chicken wire is even with the water level.

The Forster's tern lays 3 to 4 eggs that hatch after 23

43. Forster's Tern

Figure 23 (page 106)

The Forster's tern is one of the most elegant, beautiful species found on Minnesota's wetlands. These graceful, swallow-shaped birds are white with a black cap. They nest in small openings among the cattails in marshes. Typically, they will occur in a small colony of six to eight pairs, but may also be found in much larger groups.

Several nests may occur in shallow depressions on a muskrat house, and several additional nests may be comprised of small floating islands of wet marsh vegetation in the opening that occurs around the muskrat house. Such colonies usually do not need any special management to ensure their nesting success other than protection from disturbance during the nesting season. In some places in Wisconsin, however, it has been found necessary to develop a nest platform technique to ensure this bird's survival on wetlands or reservoirs that have a history of nest failure due to fluctuating water levels.

The nest platform for a Forster's tern nest is shown in Figure 23. Since the Forster's tern is a colonial-nesting species, from 10 to 20 platforms may be necessary to preserve a colony site.

Nesting platforms should be placed in existing colonies in sheltered openings among cattail vegetation. Eight-foot tall steel posts should be driven into the marsh bottom until the tops are near the high water mark, and spaced about 25 feet apart. A securing line of 1/4-inch polypropylene rope should be placed between the posts and tied at a depth of 12 inches below the water's surface. The fastening lines from each platform should be tied to the securing line at 6-foot intervals. Another technique is to anchor each fastening line to a brick that serves as an anchor. The fastening line should be long enough to prevent the platform from being submerged during periods of high water.

Once the platforms have been anchored, they can be filled with wet and decomposing marsh vegetation like that which is found on a muskrat house. An arch-like shelter of 8 to 10 dry cattail leaves are stapled onto one corner of the platform to create a shelter for the tern chicks.

This information has been provided by Mike Mossman and Randy Jurewicz of the Wisconsin Department of Natural Resources.

Table 2.
Materials needed for a Forster's Tern Nest Platform

Two ends 3/4" x 3 1/2" x 23 3/4"
Two sides 3/4" x 3 1/2" x 23 3/4"
One center brace (top) 3/4" x 1 3/4" x 23 3/4"
One center brace (bottom) 3/4" x 1 3/4" x 23 3/4"
Two end braces (bottom) 3/4" x 1 3/4" x 23 3/4"
Two styrofoam retainer strips 3/4" x 3/4" x 23 3/4"
One styrofoam panel 3/4" x 22 1/4" x 23 3/4"
Two 6" x 6" pieces of hardware cloth (1/4" mesh)
One 1/4" diameter polypropylene rope, 2 1/2'

This technique would probably also work for black terns.

Photo: Dr. Gary Neuchterlein

Individual nest platform.

This Forster's tern nest is comprised of bulrush and cattail stems and contains 3 eggs.

Photos: Wisconsin DNR

Group of Forster's tern nest platforms.

orster's terns t in wetlands of the north- entral United tes, southern ada, and even in saltwater rshes of some uthern states.

44. Cliff Swallow

Figure 24 (page 107)

The cliff swallow is one of Minnesota's most common insect-eating birds, and it is particularly abundant in northwestern parts of Minnesota. Usually it nests under the eaves of outbuildings, in culverts, on cliffs, and under bridges. The gourd-shaped nest chamber has an opening tunnel extending outward. Each nest requires one or two weeks of construction and contains 900 to 1,200 mud pellets that are carried to the site in the mouths of parent birds.

Cliff swallows can occur in colonies of hundreds of nests. Unfortunately, such colonies are subject to destruction by bridge and highway improvement projects, destruction during demolition of old buildings, and competition by English sparrows that attempt to use their nests.

If a colony is destroyed, it will probably be abandoned. However, if simulated nests are placed on the former colony site, the swallows will readily adapt to the new nests. Providing groups of such artificial nests can replace original nests at sites where a colony is destroyed by construction efforts.

The artificial nests have one other advantage: Cliff swallow pairs are more likely to raise a second brood in an artificial nest. They normally need 40 to 43 days to lay their eggs and raise their young after the nest is built. By eliminating the two-week nest building period, there is enough time for a second family to fledge.

To create a cliff swallow nest, a cliff swallow nest used by an English sparrow is selected for use as a model. (English sparrow nests are not protected by federal law). Coat the nest three times with Blue Diamond Casting Plaster. Then the entire nest is removed with a putty knife. The mud of the nest is washed out of the plaster mold. Additional plaster is added inside the mold to reduce the inside dimensions to those of a normal nest interior.

The plaster mold is then filled with liquid latex, allowed to set for about 10 minutes, and the excess latex is poured out. This leaves a thin sheet of latex over the interior of the mold. When this latex sheet has hardened, it is removed. The exterior of the latex mold is the exact duplicate of the interior of a cliff swallow nest.

The latex mold is then placed on a flat surface, front upward, and covered with a 1/4- inch layer of wet casting plaster in the manner of frosting a cake.

Prior to applying the casting is plaster, a collar of modeling clay

Photo: H. Cruickshank/VIREO

Cliff swallows make mud nests but will use artificial nests.

is set to surround the entrance hole. This collar opens outward to a diameter of approximately 2 inches. Don't cover the entrance hole with casting plaster. Any excess plaster can be trimmed with a knife before it dries. The nests can be strengthened by incorporating 1" x 6" strips of burlap into the plaster. It is easier to attach these nests to their support board if upper and lower "flanges" of plaster are created through which screws can be placed. The plaster hardens in about 15 minutes. After it has hardened, strip the flexible latex mold from inside the artificial nest. The exterior of the nest is relatively smooth in comparison to the natural nest.

The waterproof qualities of the nest can be improved by sealing the plaster with acrylic or polyurethane spray paint. The outside of the nest and the inside edge of the entrance hole are then coated with mud to simulate the real nest. This type of nest will last at least two to three years. The artificial nests are attached to boards in a horizontal line, or they can be clustered on a sheet of plywood. Nests should be in place at the site of the former colony by May 1.

This technique was provided by Melinda Welton, former endangered species supervisor of the North Carolina Wildlife Resources Commission.

45. Mallard

Figure 25 (page 108)

Nest baskets have been used for mallards for more than300 years in Great Britain and the Netherlands. The oldest form of nest basket is the pitcher-shaped basket. The original Dutch version was woven of willow shoots. The baskets were placed on islands or on the mainland on posts or in the low crotches of trees. Baskets mounted 6 feet or higher above the ground were well-used, and the entrance was tilted slightly upward.

This mallard basket idea has been modified in the Midwest into a nesting cone placed over water on a support pipe as shown in Figure 25. It was originally developed and evaluated by U.S. Fish and Wildlife Service waterfowl biologists Forrest B. Lee and Harold A. Doty of the Northern Prairie Wildlife Research Center at Jamestown, N.D. There is no universal agreement on whether or not nesting cones are really necessary for mallards because they are so adaptable. Mr. Hal Doty recommends their use only in the open prairie pothole region of the western edge of Minnesota (not forested areas). The prairie region includes Clay, Wilkin, Otter Tail, Grant, Douglas, Traverse, Stevens, Pope, and Swift counties, and perhaps some wetlands of southwestern Minnesota.

The nesting cone is a galvanized, 1/2-inch wire mesh cone, 12 inches deep with a 26-inch diameter open top. It is wired to a frame of welded, 1/4-inch diameter steel rods that are welded to a 26-inch length of pipe of a diameter that will fit snugly into the support pipe.

After assembling the basket and frame, line the inside with nesting materials. Flax straw is probably the best lining, but wild hay or small grain straw can be used. Nesting material may be placed in 2-or-3-inch-thick layers evenly within the cone and tied in place with soft, pliable wire. About 6 to 7 inches of grass should be fluffed up in the center of the basket.

A threaded hole for a setscrew should be tapped about 3 inches from the top of the support pole. The tightened setscrew prevents the basket from rotating and allows raising or lowering the basket if water levels change.

The support pole should be smooth to prevent predators like raccoons from climbing them. A 7-to 8-foot-long support pole is usually adequate unless the marsh has a very soft bottom.

Baskets are best placed in marshes that are 2 to 4 feet deep, and where water will remain at least through mid-summer. The baskets should be placed in small openings among the cattails and bulrushes, but no less than 10 feet from shore. The top of the basket should be 3 1/2 to 5 feet above the water's surface.

It is easiest to place nest baskets in winter by boring holes through the marsh ice and pounding in the support pole. Nesting baskets should be in place by April 1. They will need to be checked and maintained each subsequent year before April 1.

This information has been obtained from Art Hawkins, retired, U.S. Fish and Wildlife Service; Harold Doty; and from the publication *New Homes for Prairie Ducks* by the U.S. Fish and Wildlife Service.

Mallard nest baskets of polyethylene are also available from Dakota Waterfowl Nesting Structures, 3471 Woodland Park, Valley City, ND 58072. Phone: (701) 845-5457 and
B&K Fiberglass Rt. 2, Box 28 Garretson, SD 57030 (605) 594-6630

Part 4

Woodworking Plans to Help You Build Your Own Birdhouses

Figures 1 to 27

Figure 1

House Wren, Black-capped Chickadee*, White-breasted Nuthatch, Prothonotary Warbler, Deer Mouse, Flying Squirrel and White-footed Mouse Nest Box*

Note: Entrance hole diameter is 1 1/8".

(An entrance hole diameter of 1 1/4" is needed for the white-breasted nuthatch and flying squirrel.)

Roof — 8 1/4" × 5 1/2"

Side (2) — 8" × 5 1/2"; 1/4" holes

Floor — 4" × 5 1/2"

Front — 8" × 5 1/2"; 1"; 1 1/8"

Back — 11" × 5 1/2"

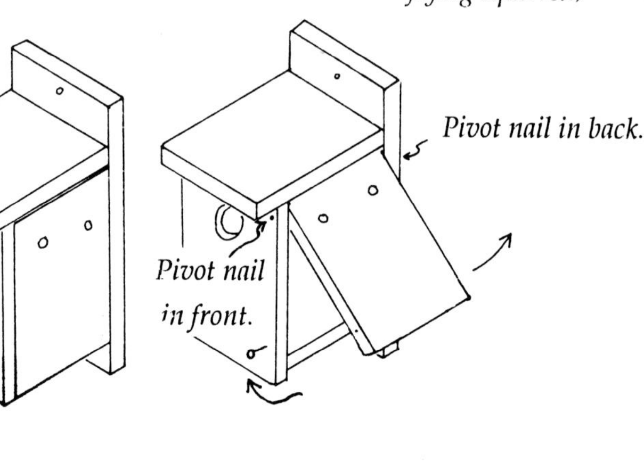

Use one nail or screw at bottom to close side. Nail or screw holds side closed.

Two "pivot" nails allow side to swing out for cleaning.

Lumber: One 1" x 6" x 4'0".

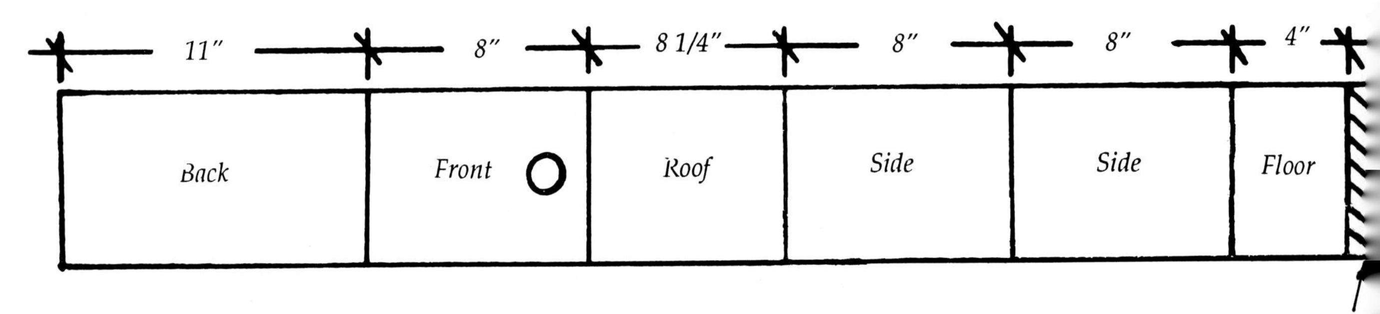

**Please note that any birdhouse entrance 1 1/4 inches in diameter or larger will admit house sparrows! All wren and chickadee nest boxes should have an entrance hole of 1 1/8 inches in diameter.*

Figure 2

Mourning Dove Nest Basket

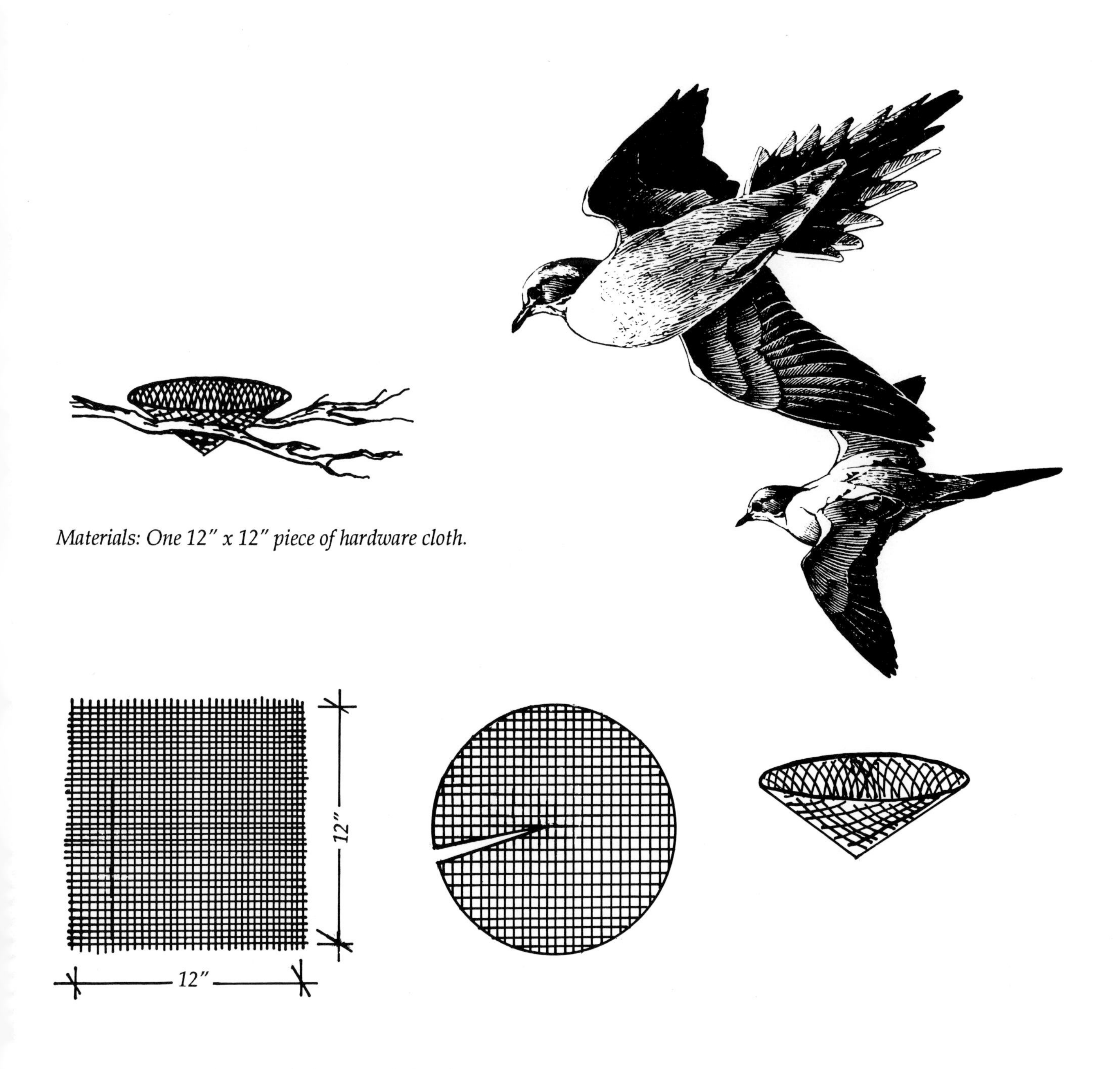

Materials: One 12" x 12" piece of hardware cloth.

Cut with tin snips to form a 12" diameter circle. Then cut to center of circle. Pull cut edges together so they overlap by 2 1/2" and wire them together to create a shallow cone. Wire and/or staple cone into the crotch of a tree limb.

Figure 3
Chickadee Winter Roost Box

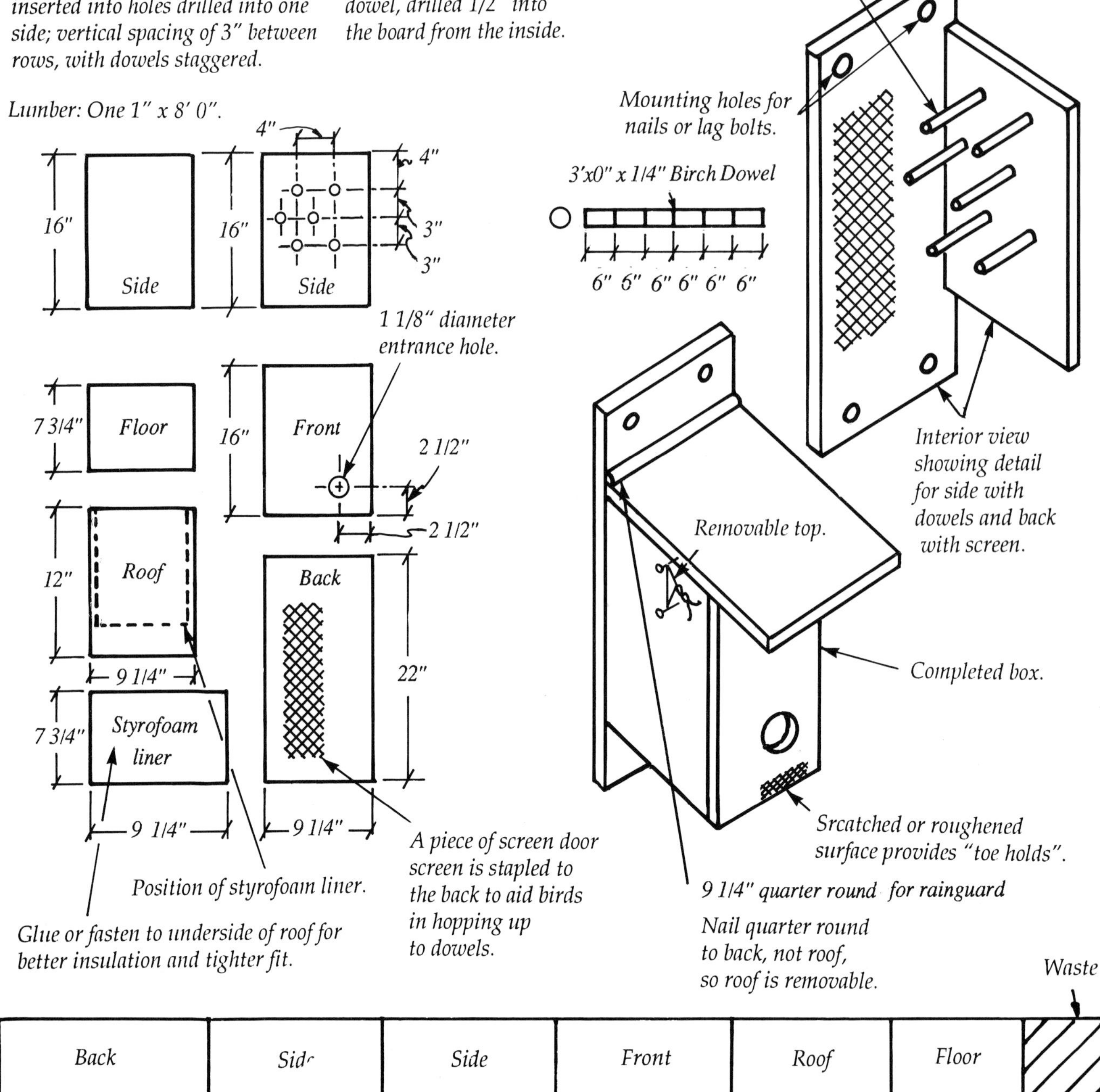

Figure 4a

Peterson Bluebird House
Materials to Build 10 Houses

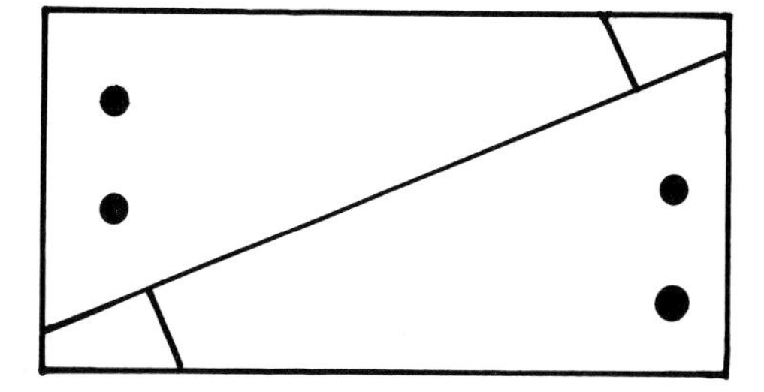

Materials:
1. One 7/16" x 12" x 16' hardboard lap siding primed (for sides).
A. Cut into 8' pieces.
B. Put two pieces finished sides together.
C. Cut into 19" pieces.
D. Trace pattern and cut.

2. One 1" x 10" x 12' rough sawn cedar (for outer roofs). Cut into 13" lengths (11 pieces).

3. One 1" x 4" x 12' rough sawn cedar (for fronts). Cut into twelve 5/8" lengths (11 pieces).

4. 30 feet 2" x 4" pine or cedar.
A. Cut to ten 2 foot lengths, angle top at 25 degrees for backs.
B. Cut inner roof and floor pieces - takes approximately one foot per house.

To assemble - use either cement coated 8d nails or 1 7/8" ring shank flooring nails.

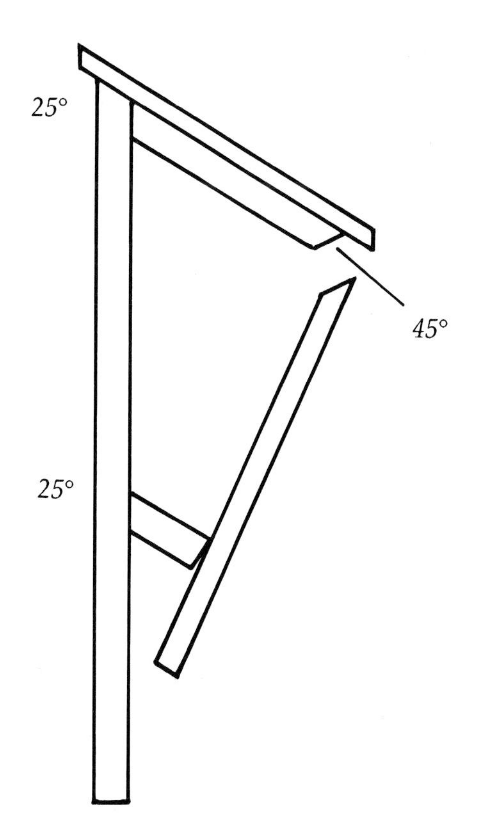

If you would like to purchase kits or assembled houses, call or write:
Ahlgren Construction
Dave & Jan Ahlgren
12989 Otchipwe Avenue North
Stillwater, MN 55082
612-430-0031.

To save shipping and packing you can pick up in Stillwater at "THE BIRD HOUSE", 5901 Omaha Avenue North, across from the Stillwater K-Mart store. Phone 612-439-1923 to be sure they have what you need in stock. Hours are: 9:30 to 5:30, Monday through Saturday.

Figure 4b

Peterson Bluebird House
(See page 83 for details on making 10 houses at a time)

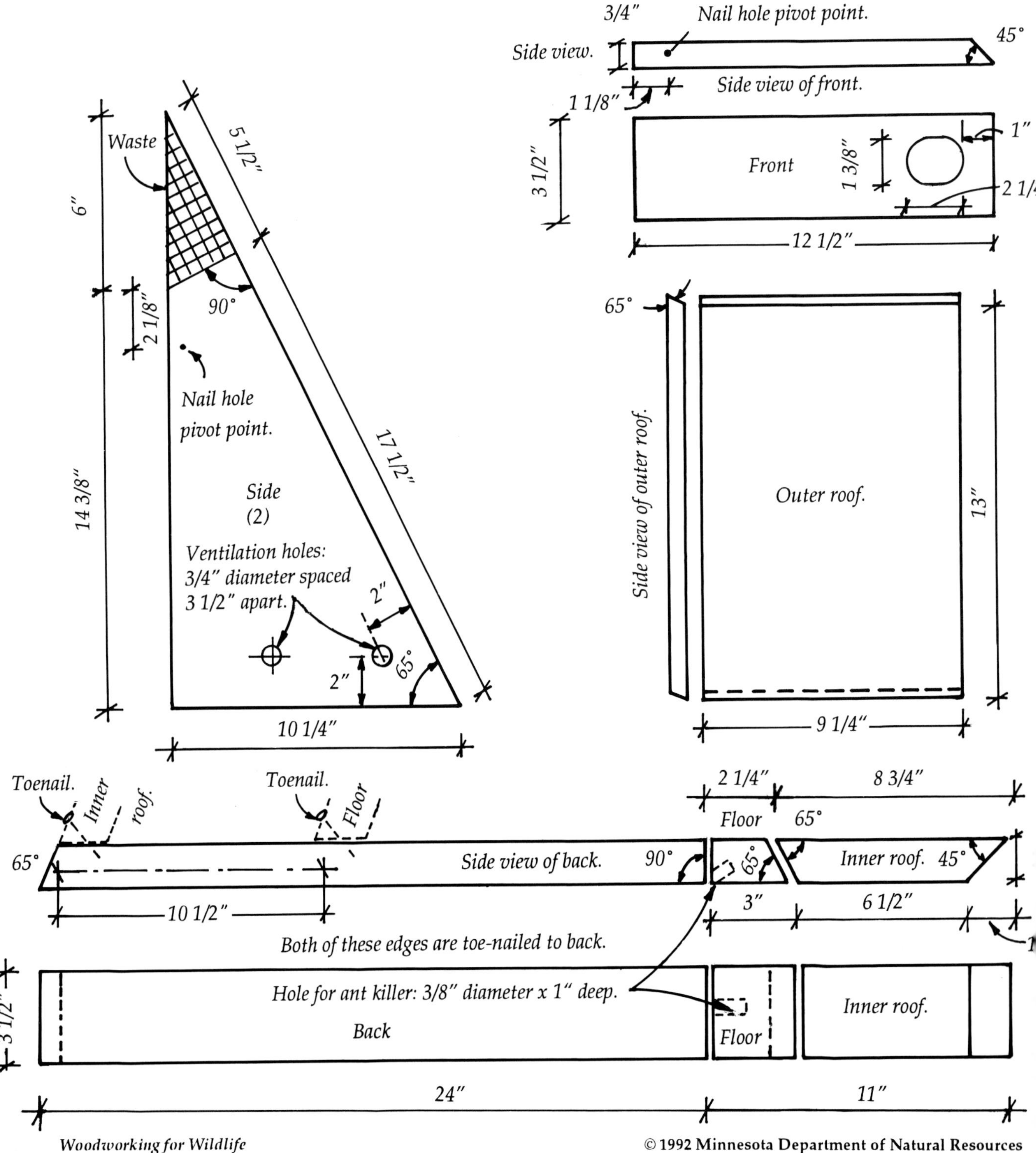

Figure 4b

Peterson Bluebird House (Continued)

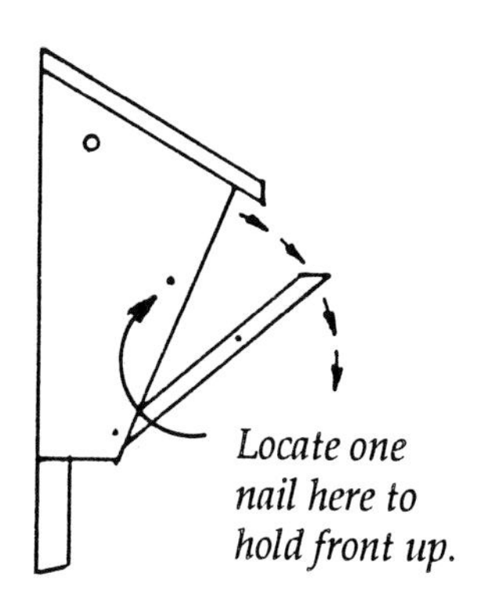

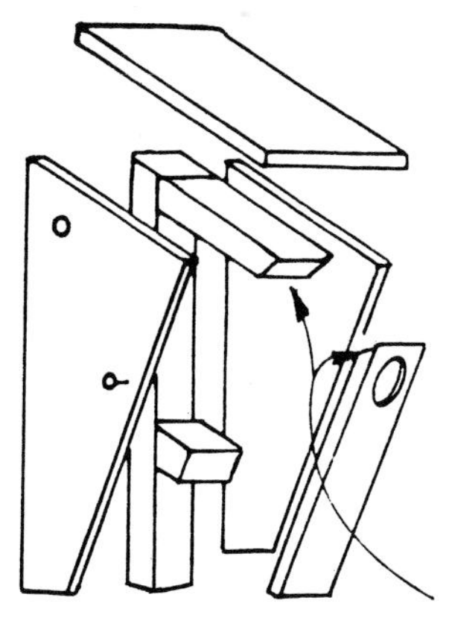

The most commonly known bluebird house is a rectangular house with a 1 1/2" diameter entrance hole. A hole any larger will admit European starlings. This house is relatively easy to make, but it should be on a predator-proof post to avoid predation by cats.

But probably the best all-around design is the Peterson bluebird house, developed by Dick and Vi Peterson of Brooklyn Park, Minnesota after experience with over 3500 bluebird houses.

It meets all the requirements of a bluebird house. The front opens for easy cleaning. The sloping roof with wide overhang discourages cats.

There are provisions for insulation, ventilation, drainage, and ant control.

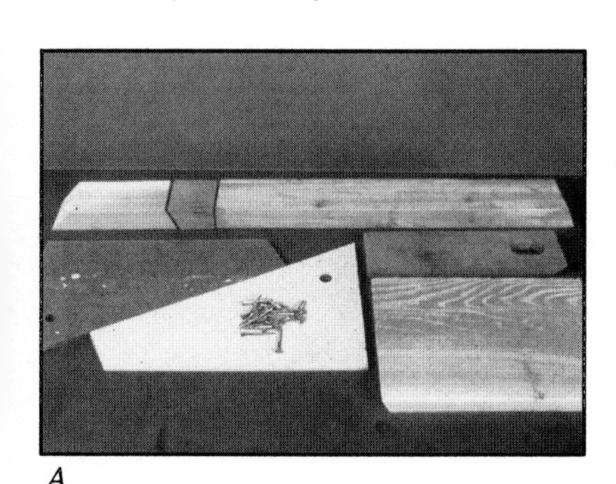
A

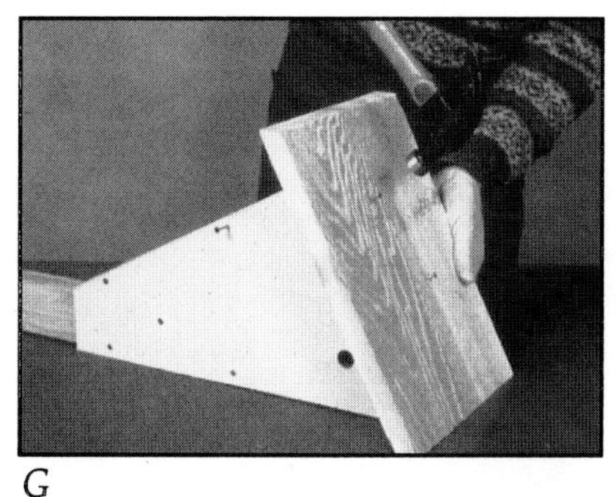
G

A. The Peterson house has seven parts and is assembled in this order:

B. The inner roof is toe-nailed to the back.

C. Then, the floor is toe-nailed to the back.

D. Third, one side is nailed to the resulting frame.

E. Then the other side is nailed to the frame.

F. Next the swing-down front is fastened by a nail into each side. A third nail is pounded part-way into the side near the entrance hole. This is removed each time the house is checked.

G. Finally, the outer roof is nailed on top.

B

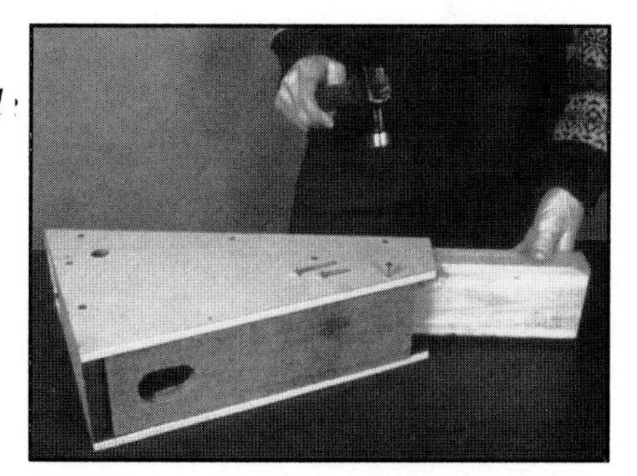
F

C

D

E

Figure 5

Tree Swallow, Eastern Bluebird, and Great Crested Flycatcher Nest Box

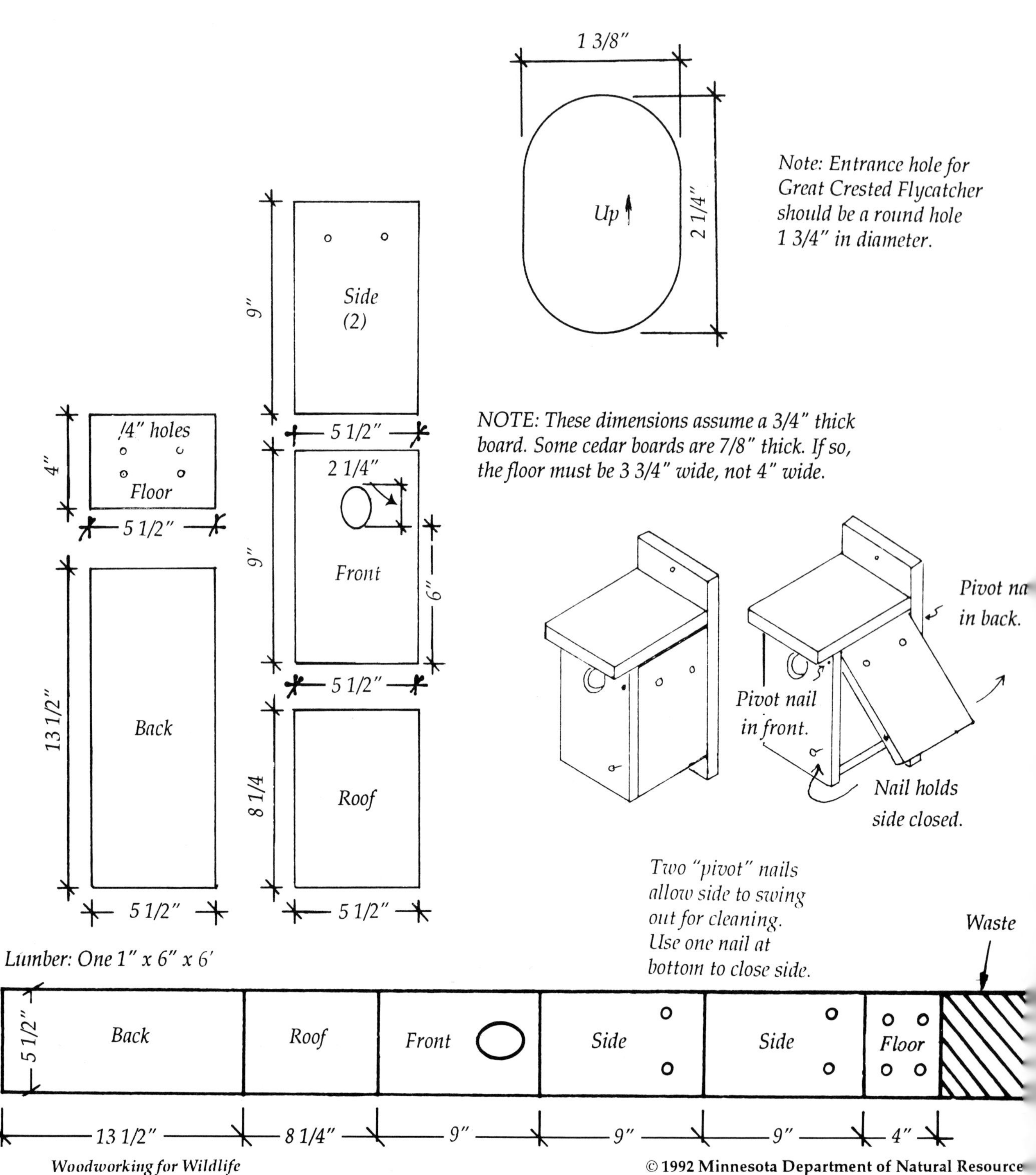

Figure 6

American Robin, Barn Swallow, and Eastern Phoebe Nest Shelf

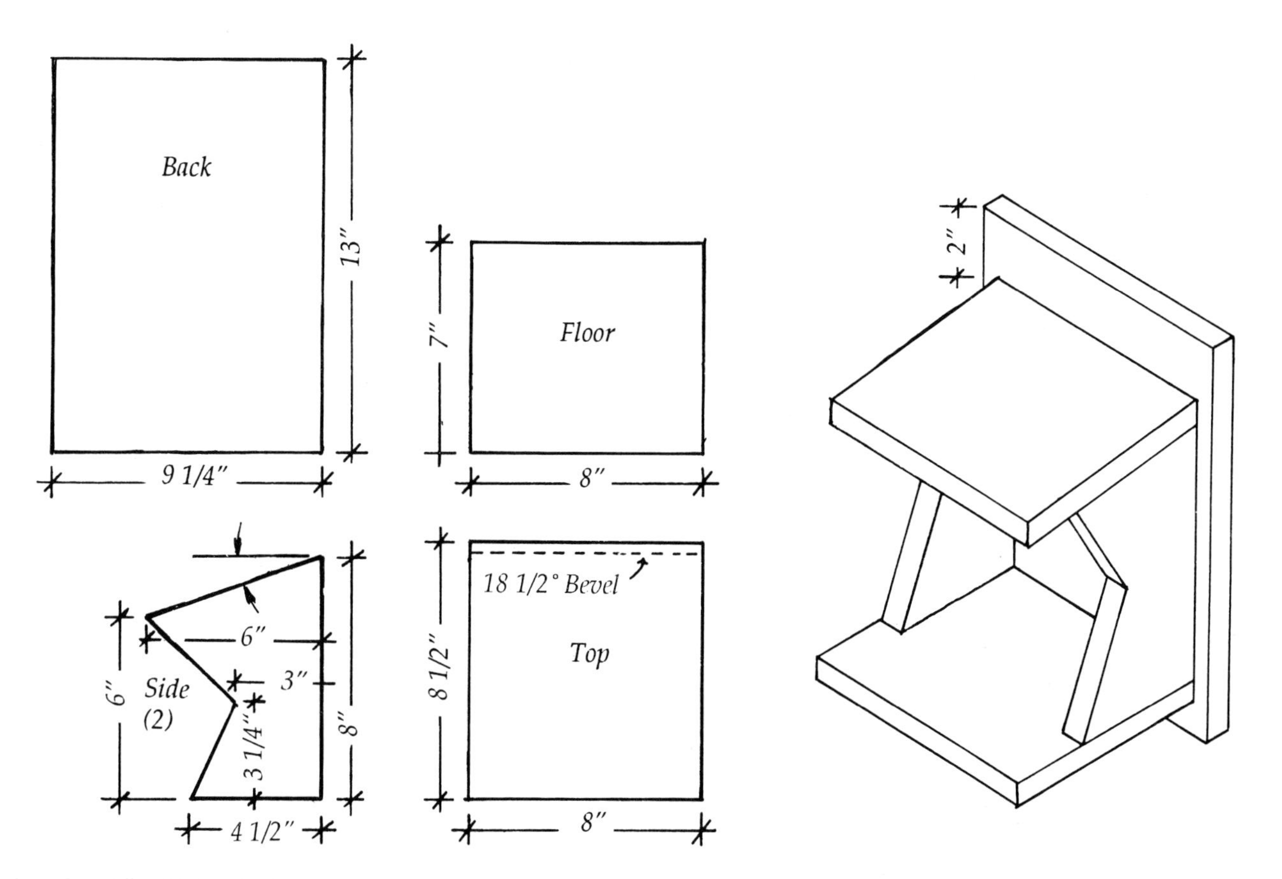

Lumber: One 1″ x 10″ x 4′ 0″.

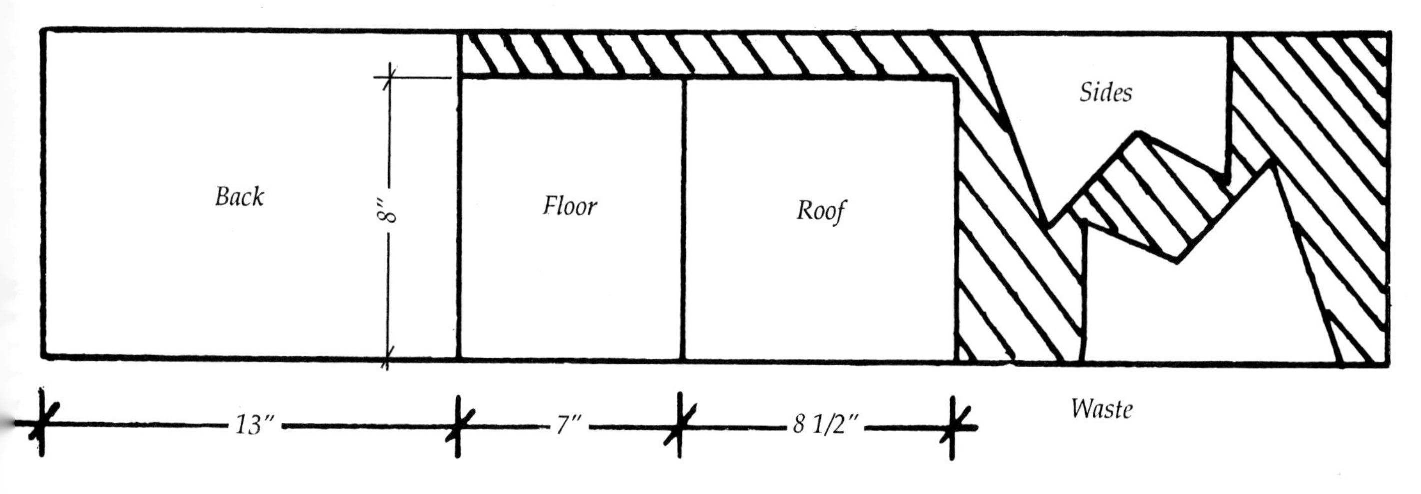

Figure 7

Purple Martin House

Materials:
4′ x 8′ x 1/4″ plywood.
2″ x 2″ x 6″ for chimney.
1″ x 2″ x 14′ for base.
1″ x 1″ x 8′ for corner blocks.
4″ x 8″ metal window screen.
4″ x 4″ x 14′ cedar post.

Place 1/2″ dowel railing around balcony to keep young from falling.

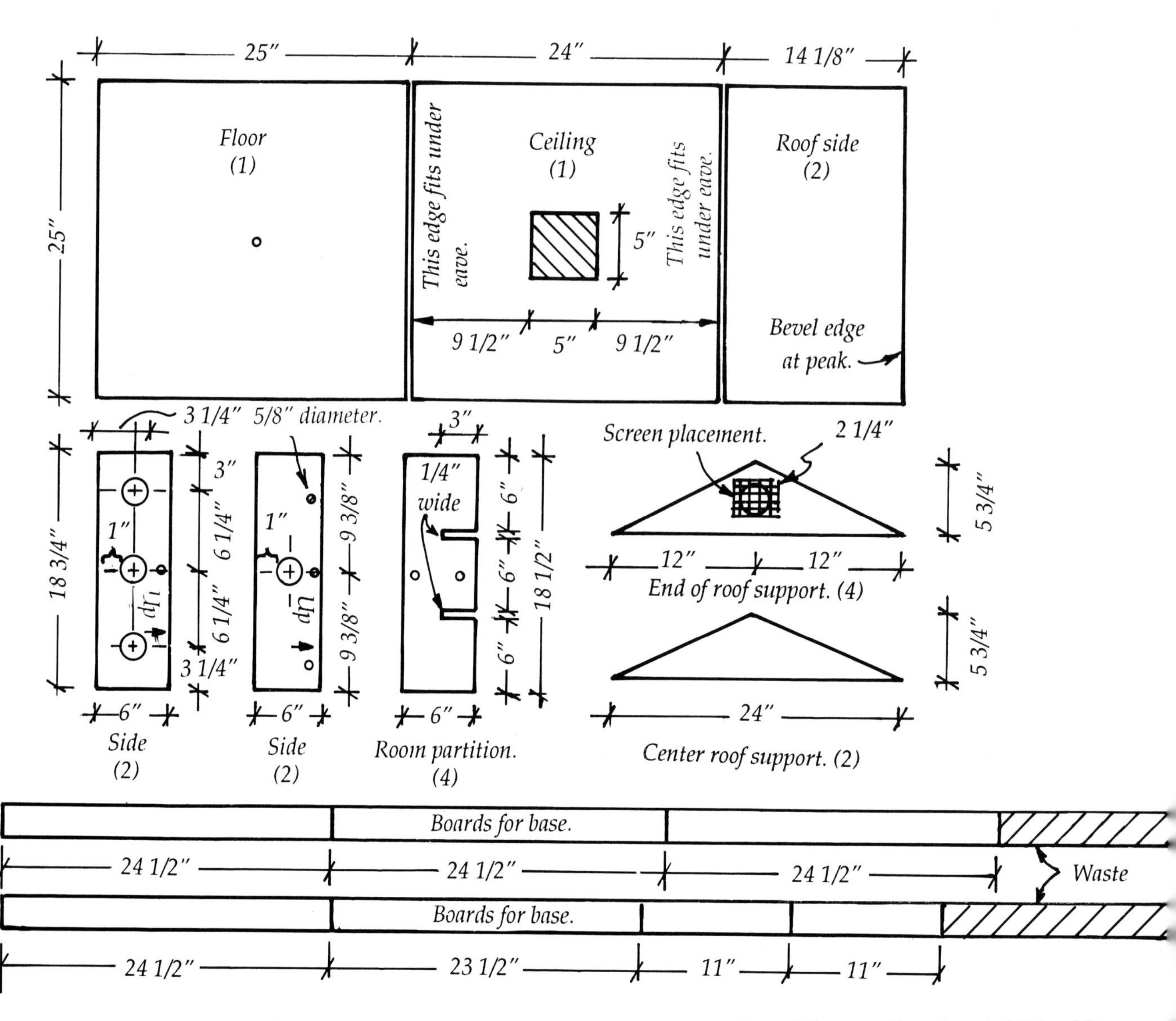

Figure 7

Purple Martin House (Continued)

This pattern shows how to cut out a martin house from one sheet of plywood.

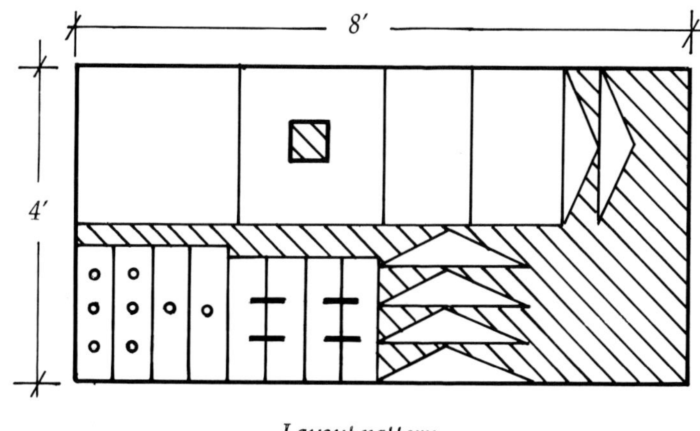

Layout pattern.

Expanded view of Martin House. A threaded rod inserts through the base and up through the chimney.

Entrance hole diameter: 2 1/4″.

Locate 5/8″ ventilation holes 1″ below top edge of sides.

** For sides, measurement from floor to center of entrance holes = 2 1/8″.*

Note: This plan is for a one-story house. To add a second story, make one more ceiling unit (25″ x 25″), four more sides, and four more room partitions.

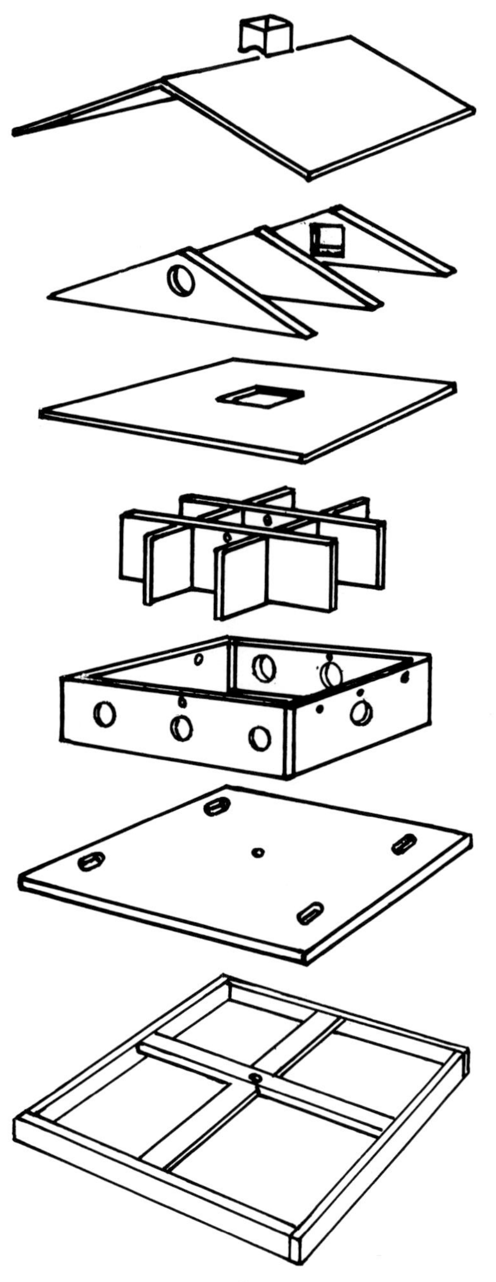

Figure 8
Northern Flicker Nest Box

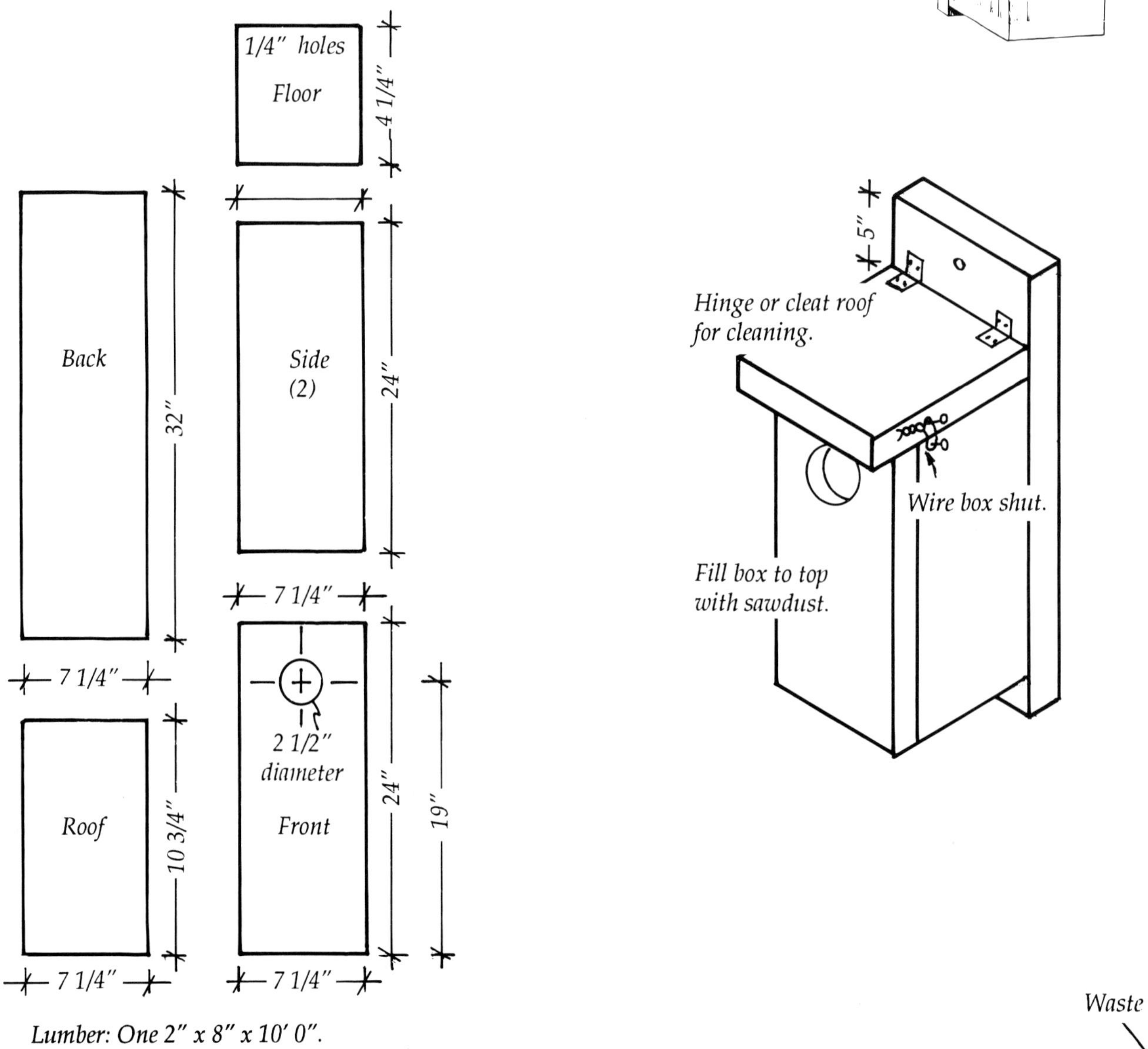

Figure 9
Johnson Bat House

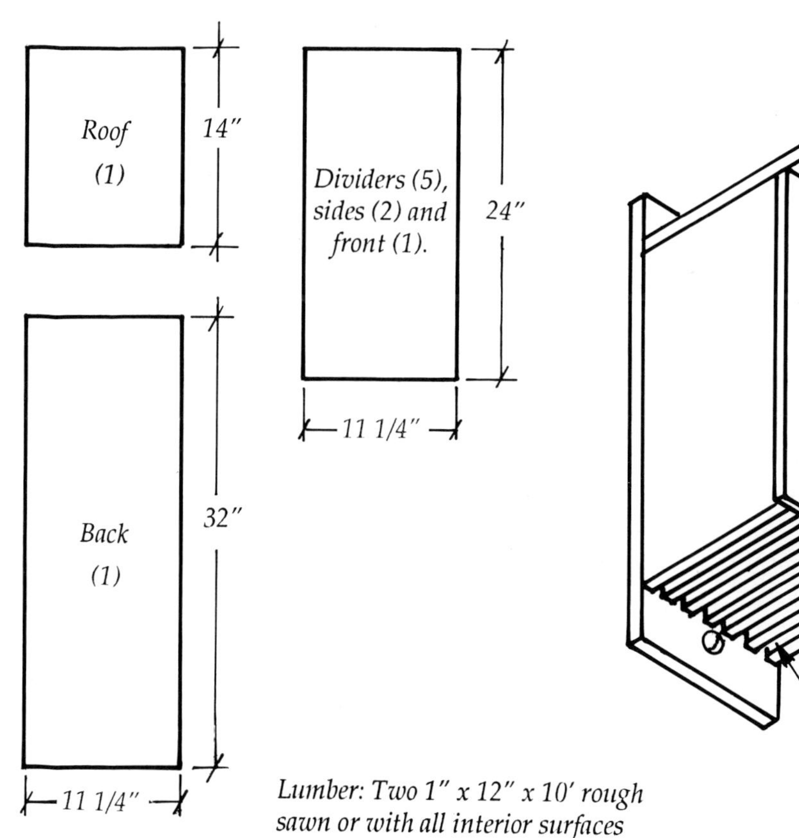

Lumber: Two 1" x 12" x 10' rough sawn or with all interior surfaces roughened.

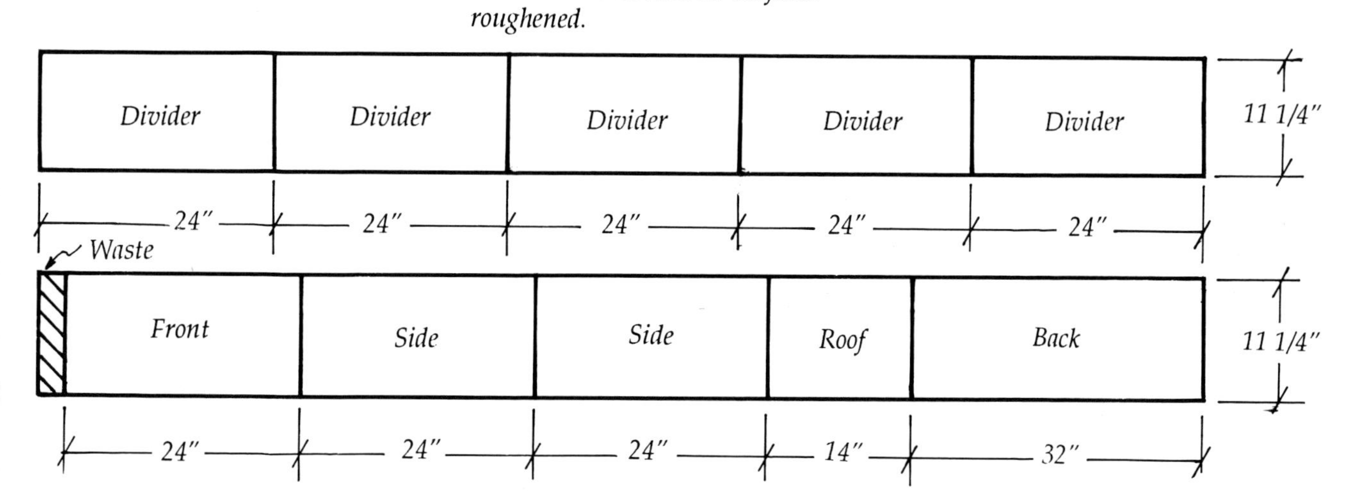

Note: All external seams and joints should be caulked if not tight fitting. Divider boards are spaced 1 inch apart.

Figure 10
Small Bat House

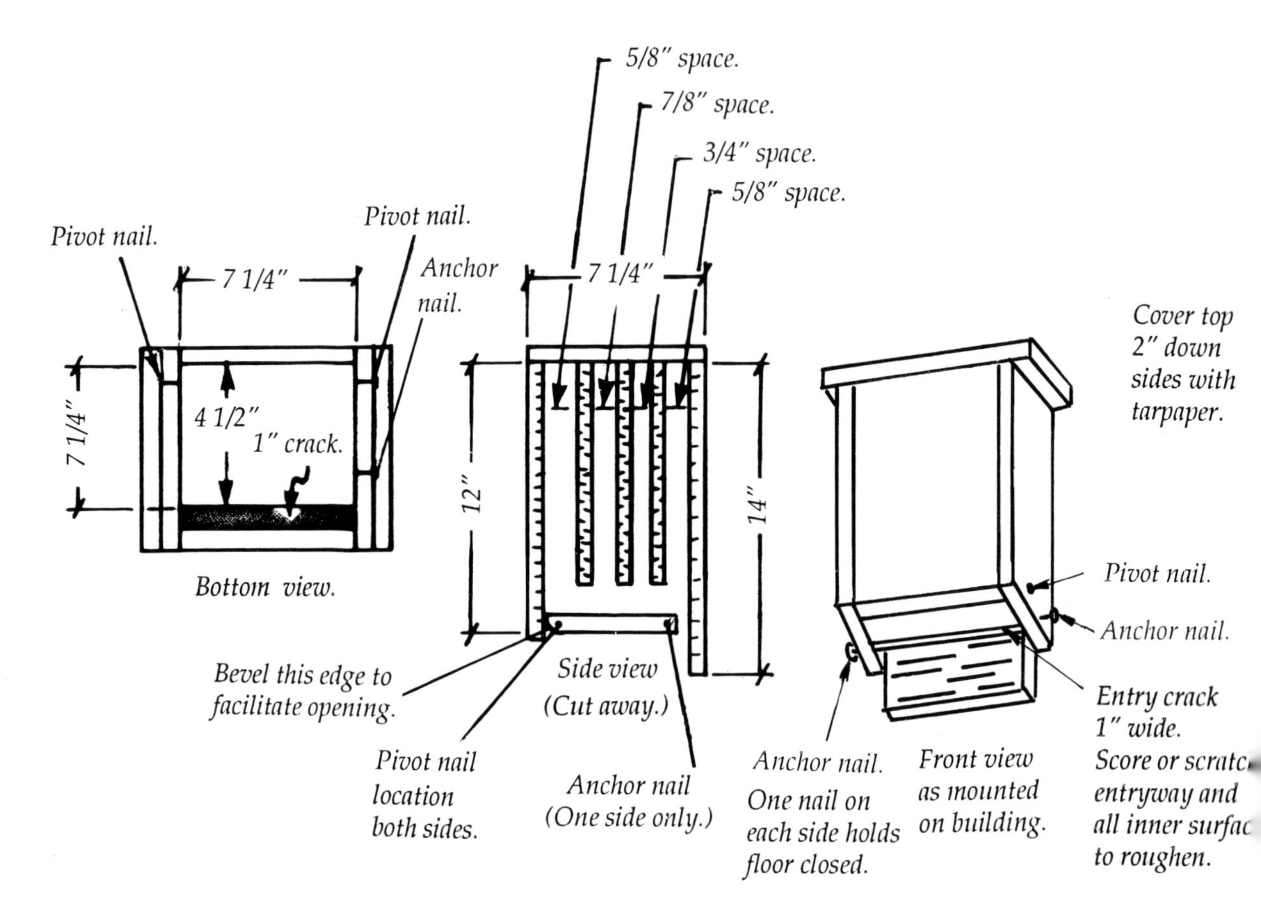

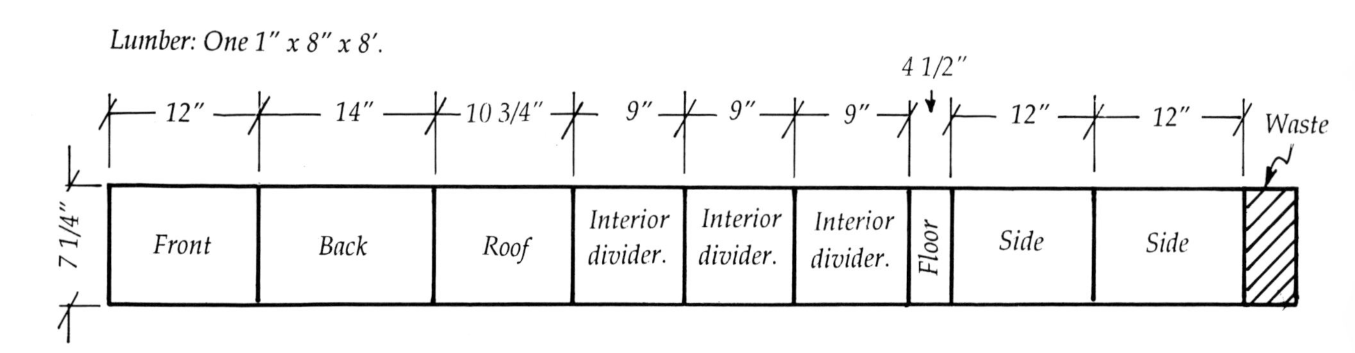

Figure 11
Burrowing Owl Nest Tunnel

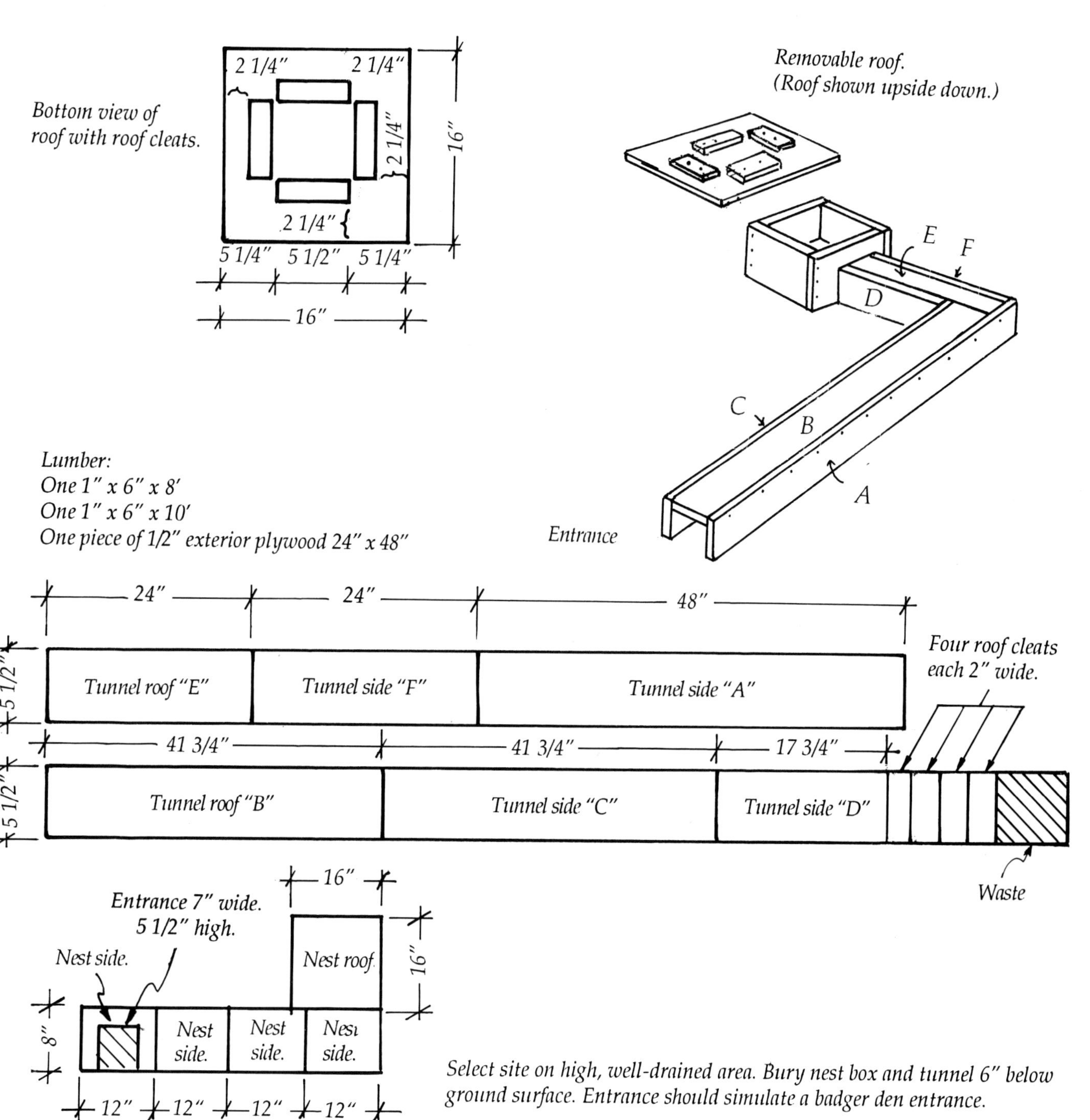

Select site on high, well-drained area. Bury nest box and tunnel 6" below ground surface. Entrance should simulate a badger den entrance.

Figure 12

Barred Owl Nest Box

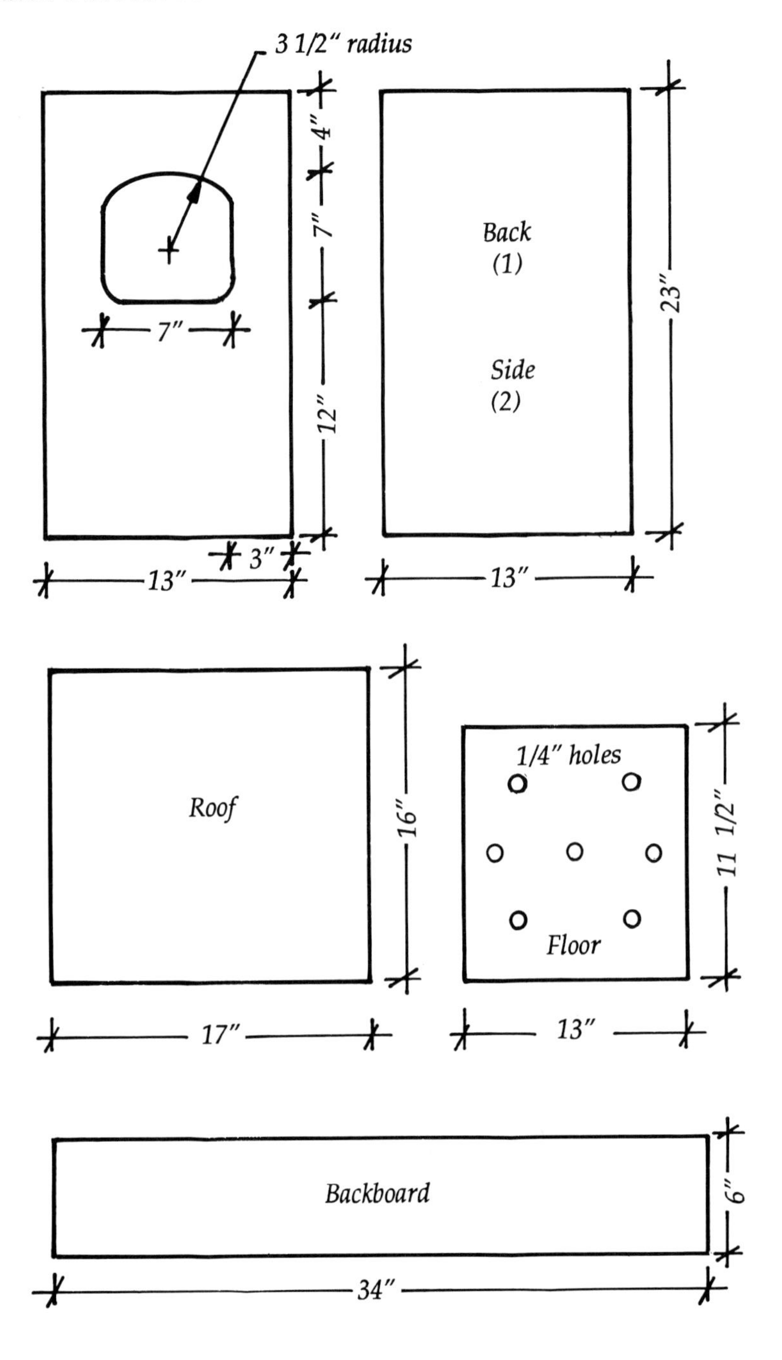

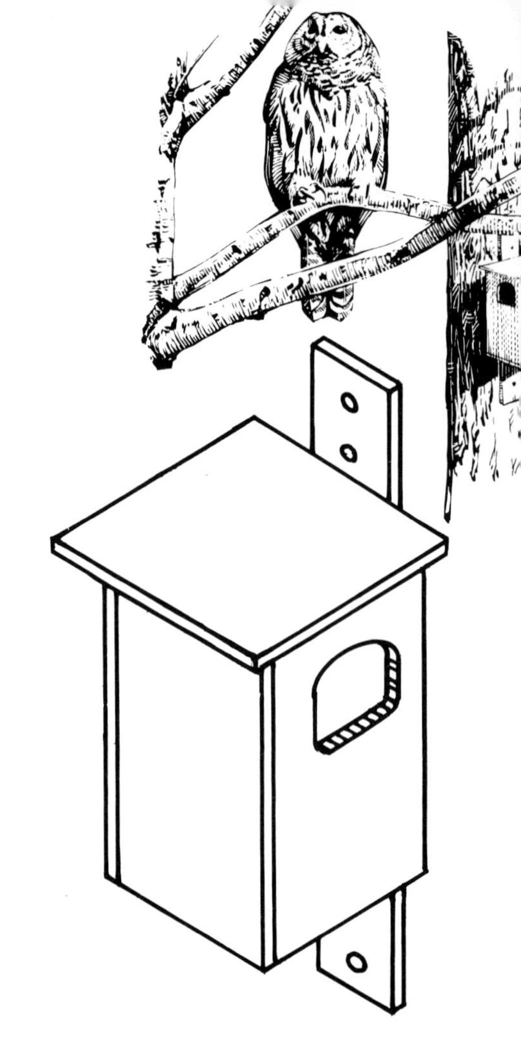

Note: No hinged door needed. Clean through entrance hole.

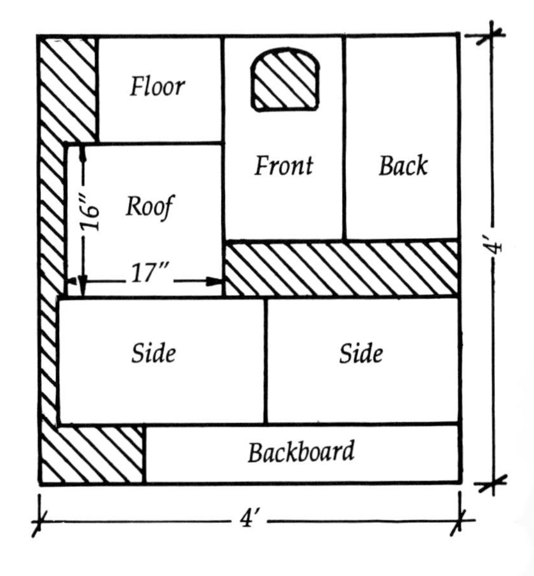

Lumber: One 4' x 4' x 3/4" sheet exterior plywood.

Figure 13

American Kestrel, Northern Screech-owl, Northern Saw-whet Owl, Boreal Owl, Gray Squirrel, Red Squirrel, and Fox Squirrel Nest Box

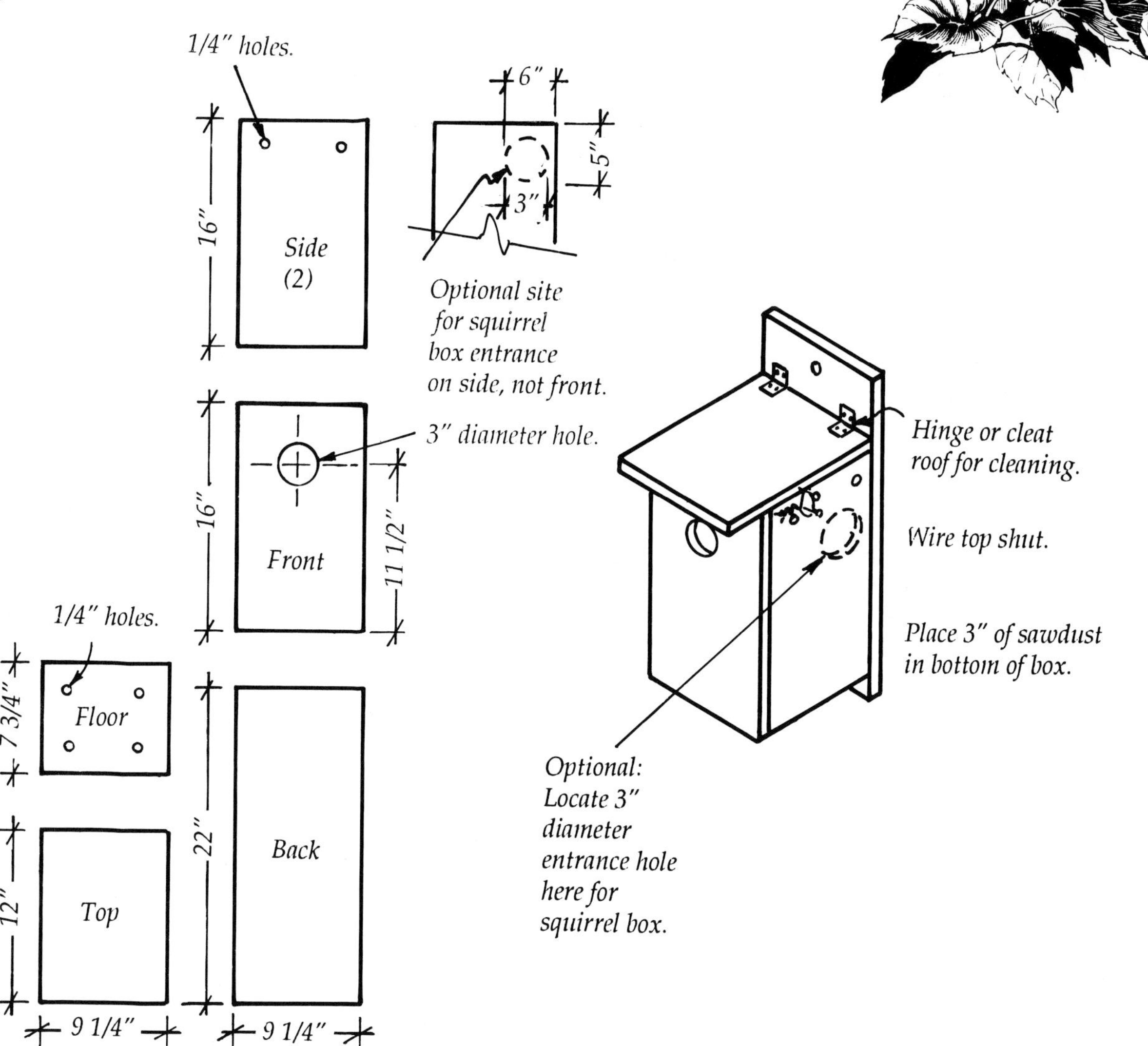

Lumber: One 1″ x 10″ x 8′ 0″

Back	Side	Side	Front	Top	Floor
22″	16″	16″	16″	12″	7 3/4″

Figure 14

Great Gray Owl and
Great Horned Owl Nest Platform

Materials:
One square yard 1 inch mesh chicken wire.
One square yard tarpaper.

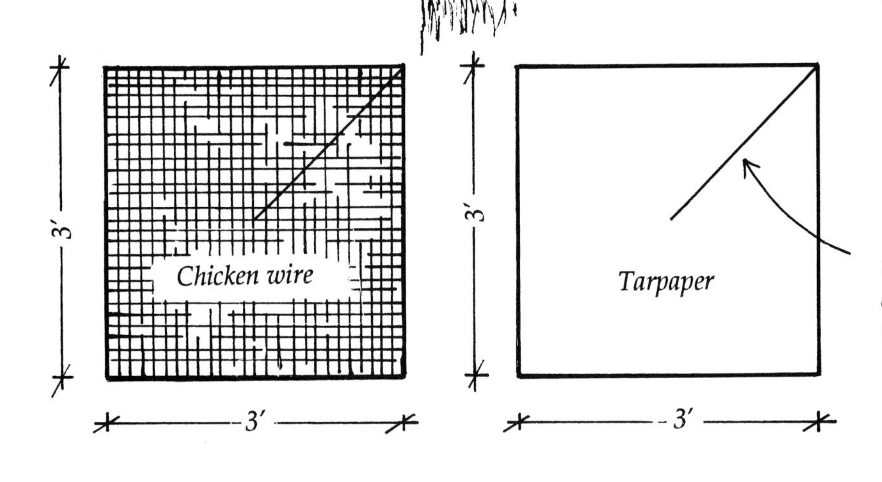

Cut along these lines and overlap edges to make a cone 14″ deep.

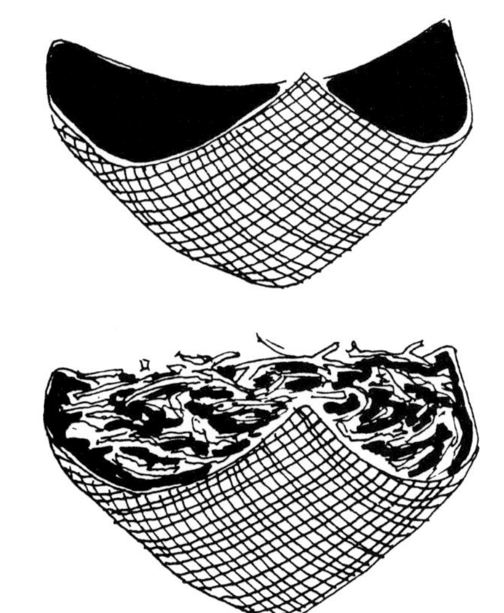

Line inside of wire cone with tarpaper.

Cut drain hole in bottom.

Construct stick nest inside cone, wiring branches to cone through tarpaper.
Raise finished nest into tree with rope and wire into a crotch of the tree.

Figure 15

Barn-Owl Nest Box for Inside a Covered Silo (This design has a front section with entrance hole.)

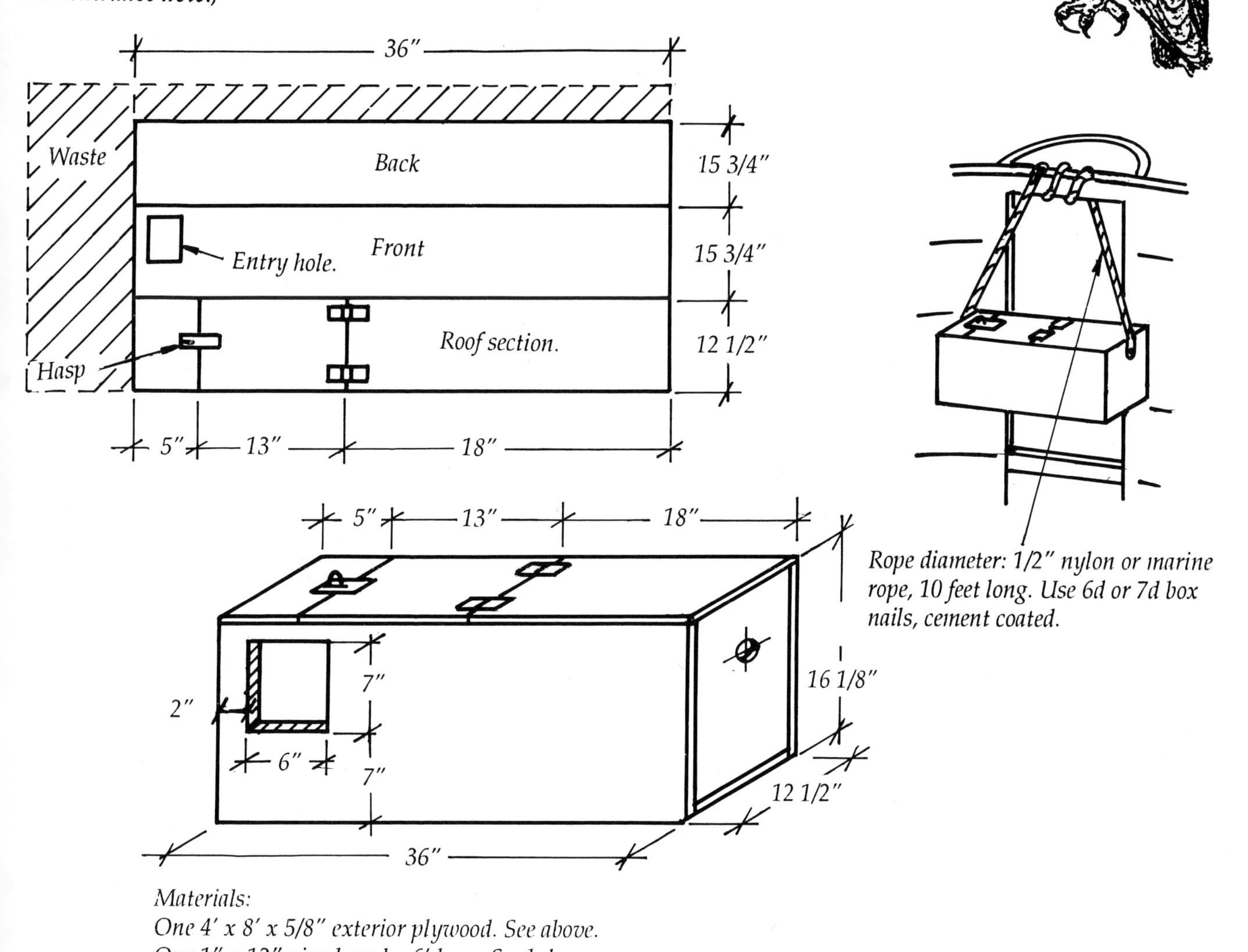

Rope diameter: 1/2" nylon or marine rope, 10 feet long. Use 6d or 7d box nails, cement coated.

Materials:
One 4' x 8' x 5/8" exterior plywood. See above.
One 1" x 12" pine board x 6' long. See below.

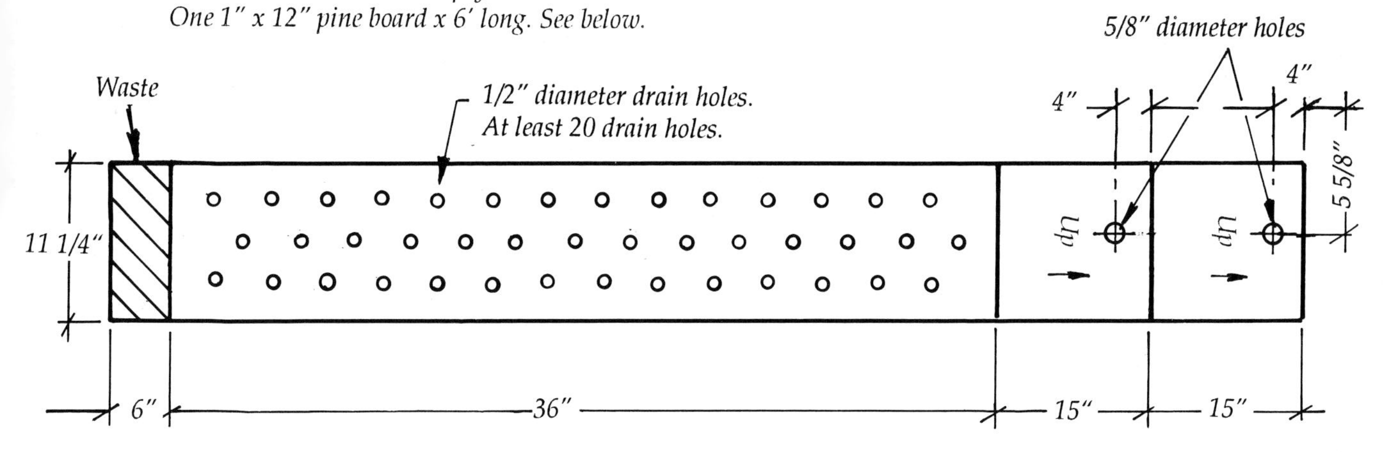

Figure 16

Barn Owl Nest Box for Inside a Hay Loft Wall (This design does not include a front section, and the Roof Section is 11 7/8" wide instead of 12-1/2" wide)

Side view of nest box for use against barn wall.

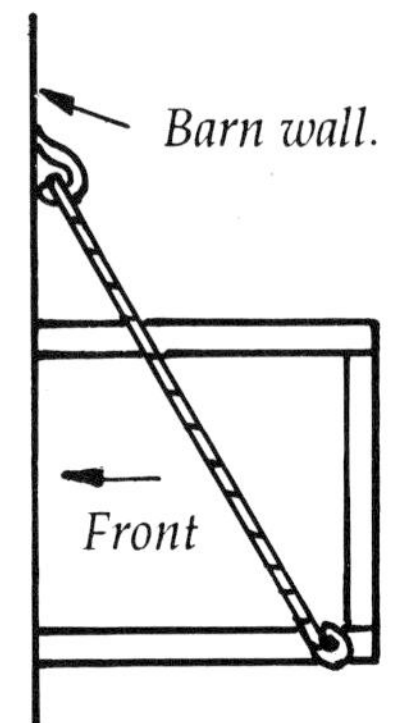

Roof and floor boards should enclose back.

Although any barn can be used, the best building in which to install a barn owl nest box is an abandoned or seldom used barn on a farmstead.

Select the "clean face" or end of a barn having few or no openings.

Choose a crossbeam on which to mount the box.

Cut a 6" x 6" hole in the barn wall, providing a direct entrance into the box from the outside barn.

The entrance hole should be 20 to 25 feet above the ground.

Mount the box by nailing it to the beam.

Provide additional support as necessary by bracing the box with 2" x 4" lumber or by attaching wire or rope from the lower outside corners to the wall.

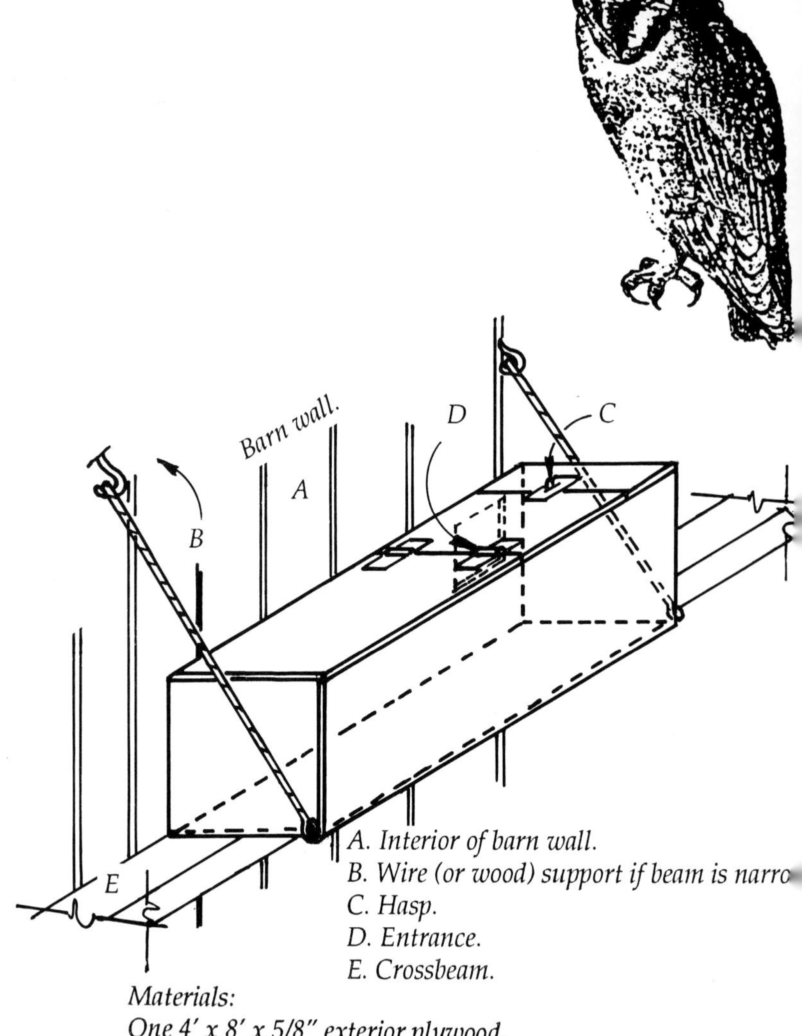

Materials:
One 4' x 8' x 5/8" exterior plywood.
One 1" x 12" x 6' pine board.

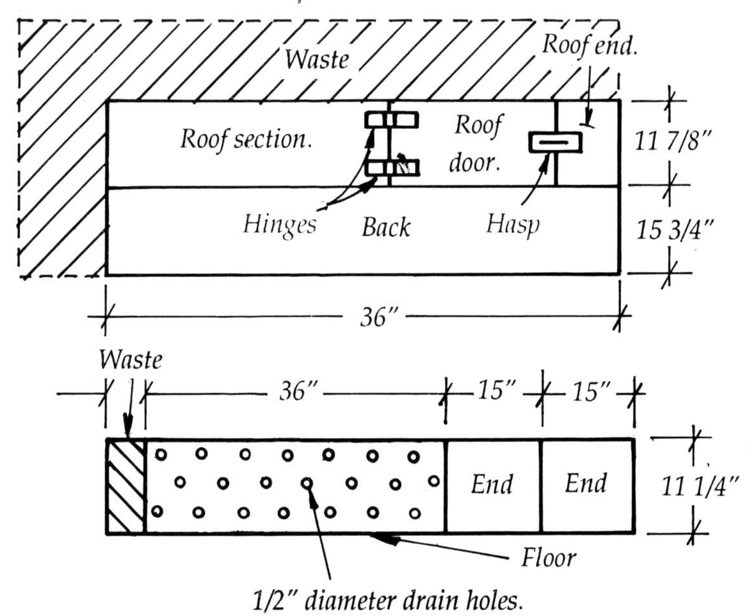

Figure 17

Common Merganser, Raccoon, and Pileated Woodpecker Nest Box

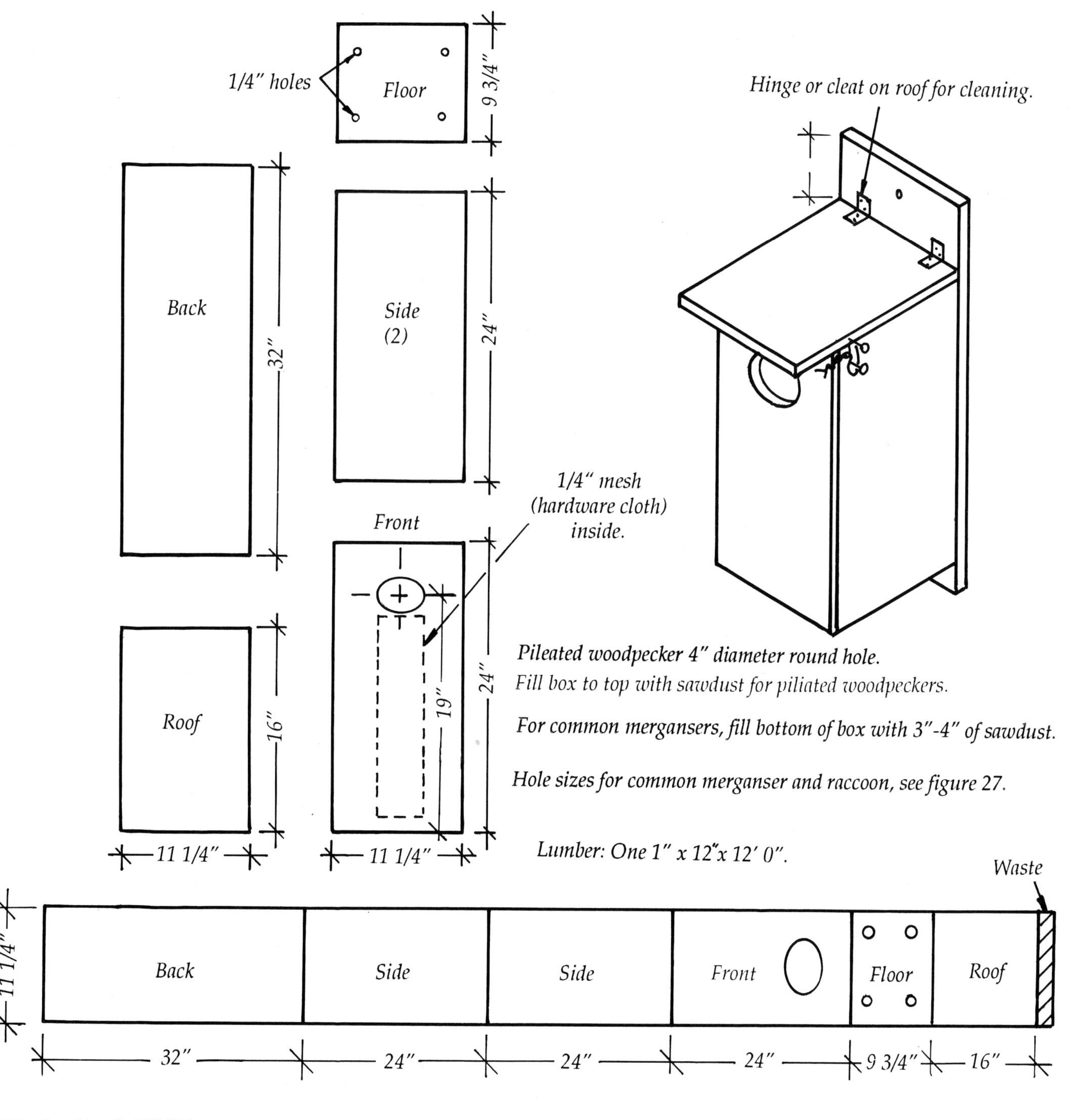

Figure 18

Wood Duck, Hooded Merganser, and Common Goldeneye Nest Box (This design developed by Don "Duckman" Helmeke)

KESTREL NOTE: This design will also work well for American kestrels if you use a 3" diameter entrance hole centered 4 1/2" down from the top edge of the front.

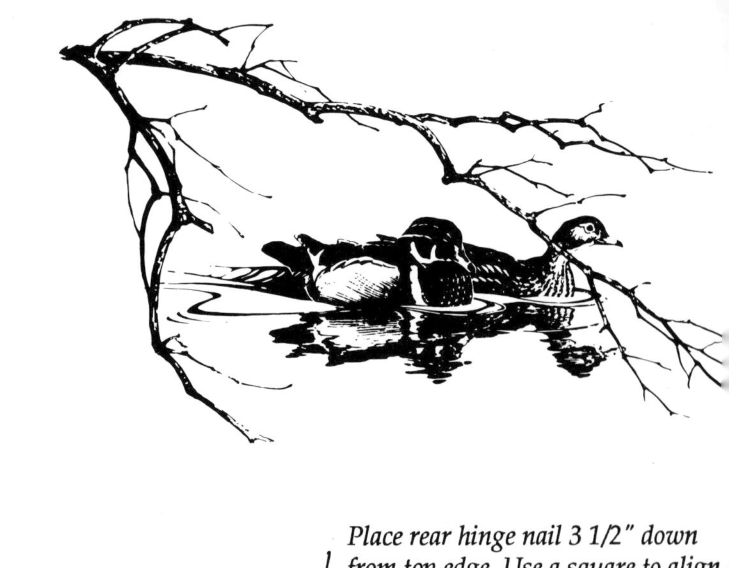

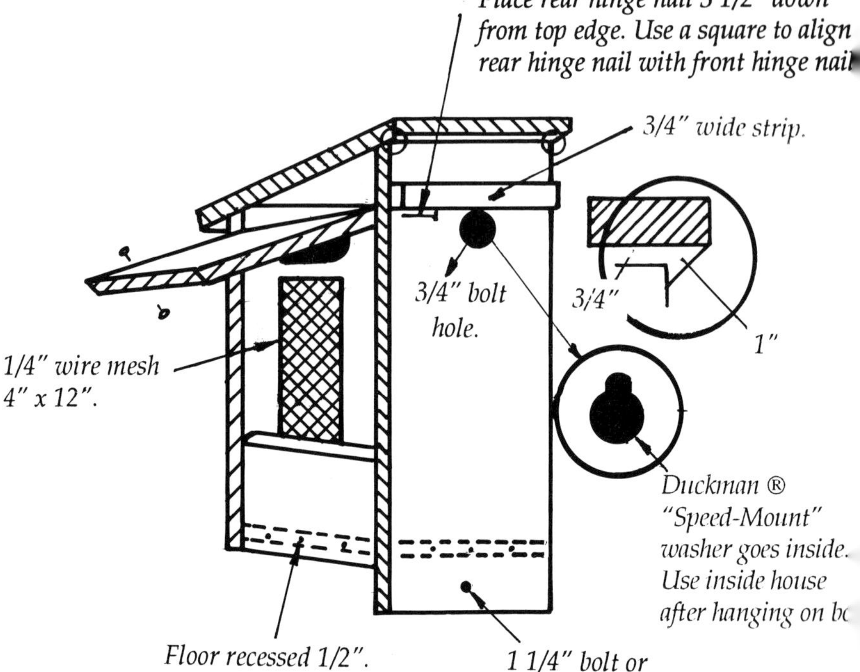

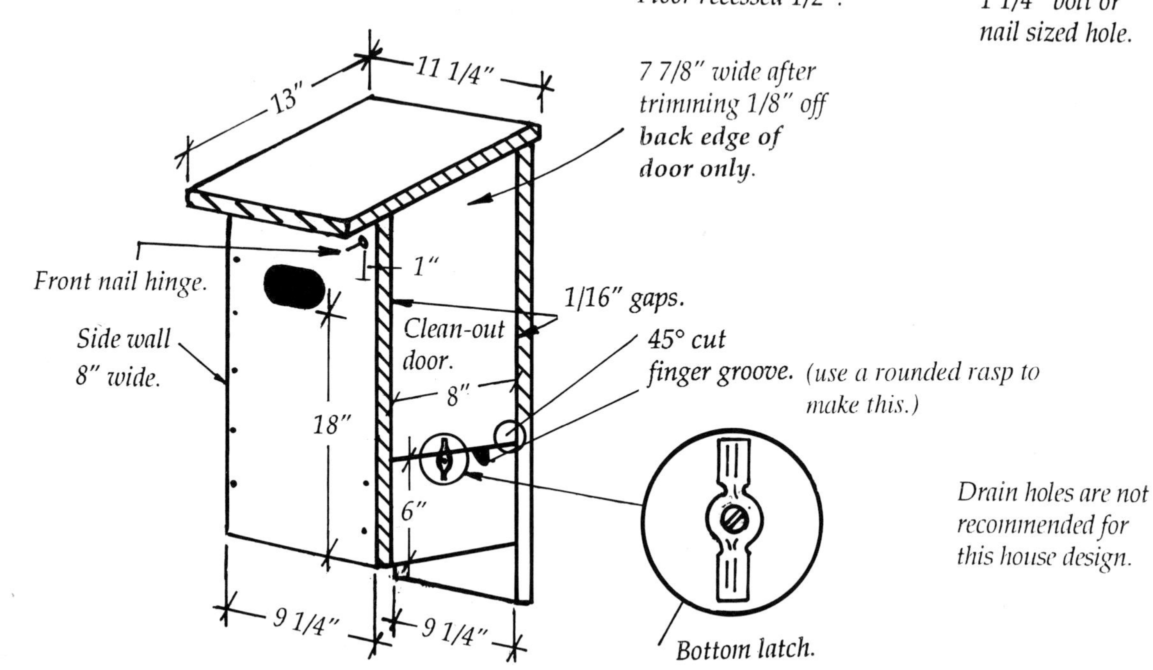

Figure 18

Wood Duck, Hooded Merganser, and Common Goldeneye Nest Box (Continued)

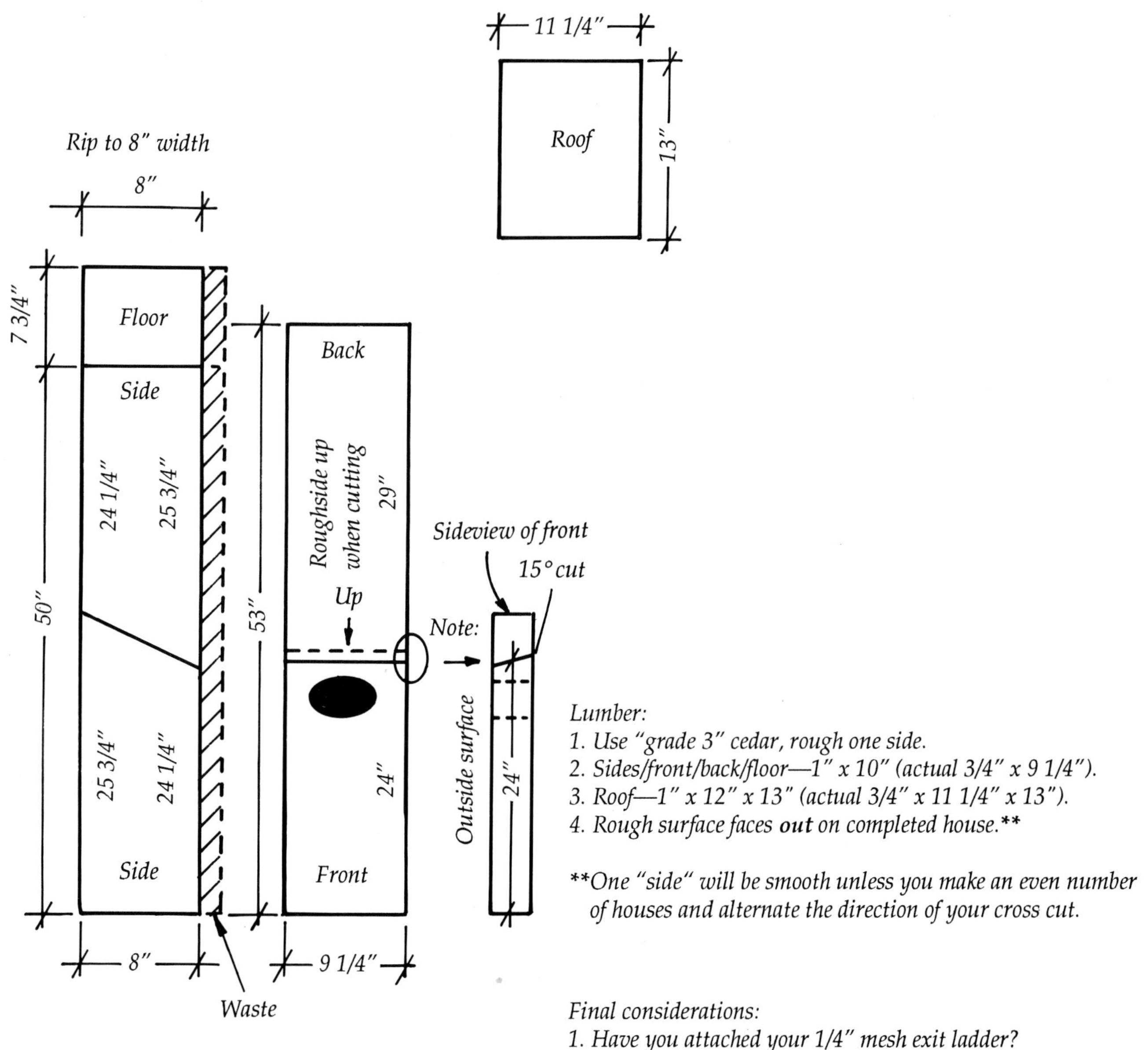

Lumber:

1. *Use "grade 3" cedar, rough one side.*
2. *Sides/front/back/floor—1" x 10" (actual 3/4" x 9 1/4").*
3. *Roof—1" x 12" x 13" (actual 3/4" x 11 1/4" x 13").*
4. *Rough surface faces **out** on completed house.***

***One "side" will be smooth unless you make an even number of houses and alternate the direction of your cross cut.*

Final considerations:

1. *Have you attached your 1/4" mesh exit ladder? Uea a staple gun to attach.*
2. *Add 4" of cedar shavings as nest base material.*

Figure 19
Common Loon Nest Platform

Chick ramp: It is important to fasten a gently sloping ramp from the side of the platform into the water to allow loon chicks to climb back onto the platform after their first swim.

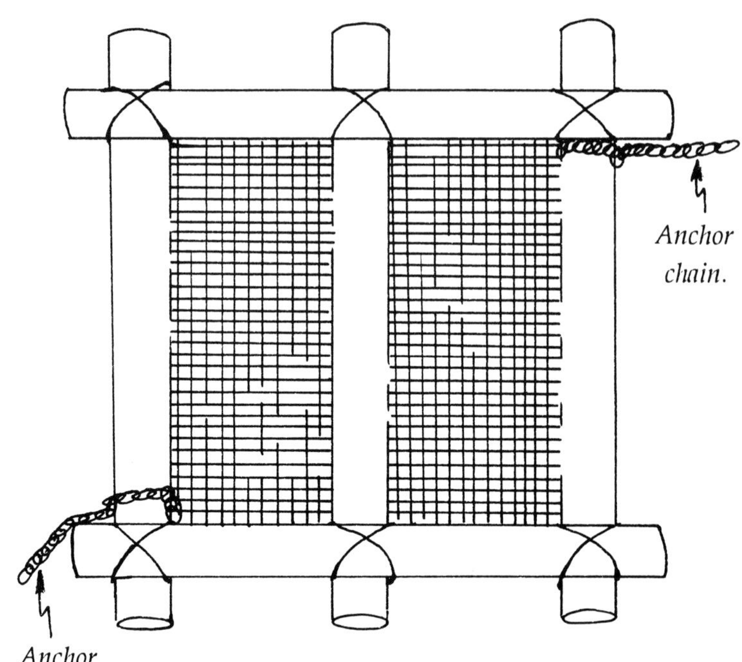

Materials:
Five 10" diameter cedar poles - 6 feet long.
One 4' x 4' welded wire screen (2" x 4" mesh).

Notch logs and latch together with wire.
Staple wire screen under raft.
Fill raft with wet aquatic vegetation.
Anchor with chains at opposite corners.

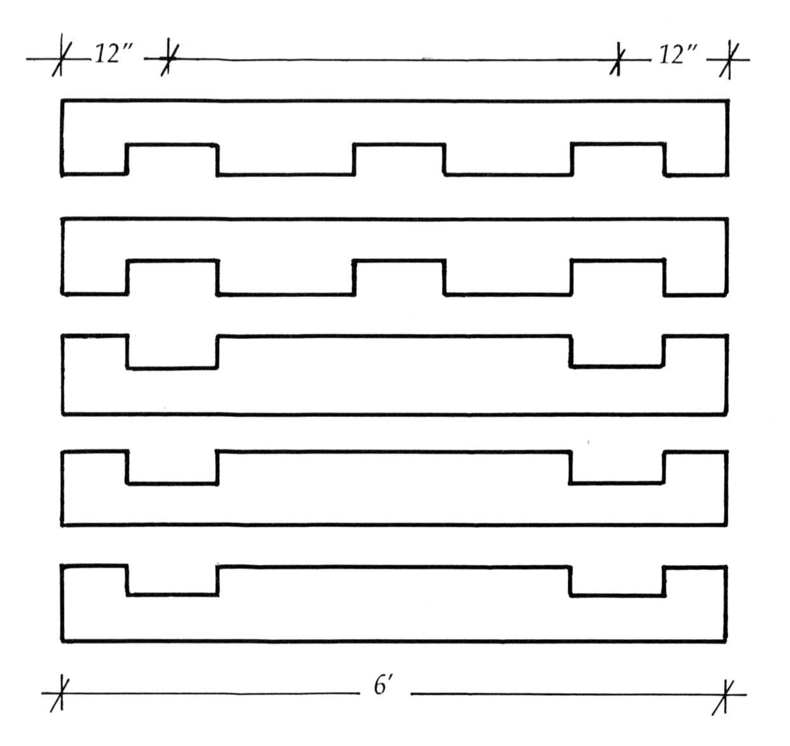

Figure 20

Great Blue Heron, and Double-crested Cormorant Nest Platform

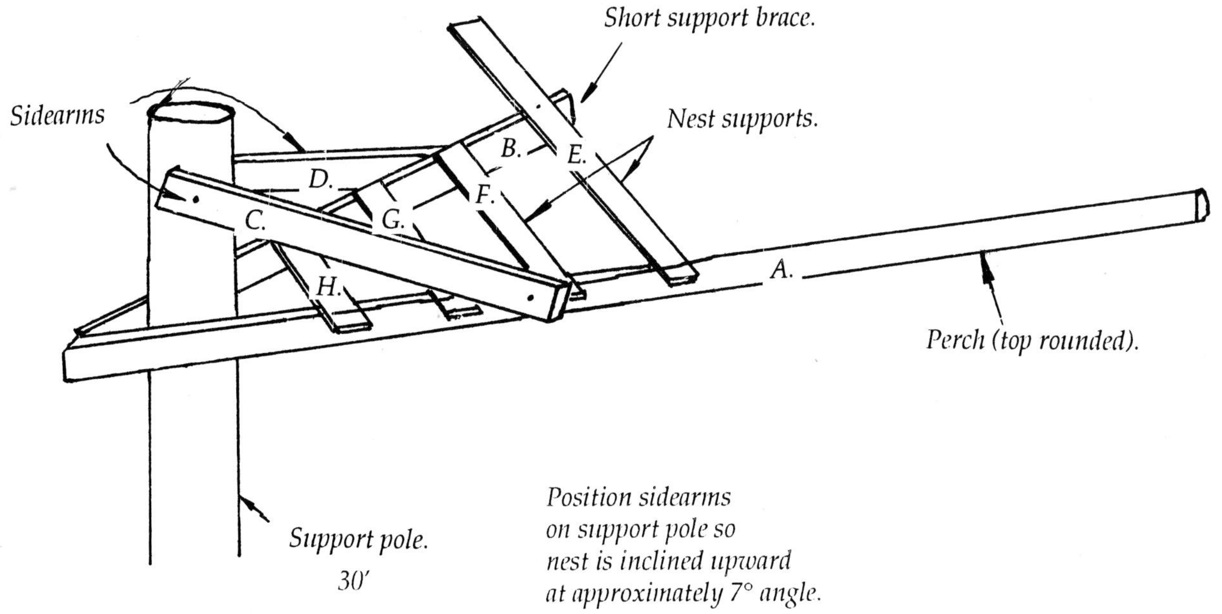

Position sidearms on support pole so nest is inclined upward at approximately 7° angle.

Wire armful of sticks onto lath nest supports to stimulate use.

Lumber:
A. 2″ x 2″ x 7′.
B. 2″ x 2″ x 30″.
C. 1″ x 2″ x 26 1/2″.
D. 1″ x 2″ x 26 1/2″.
E. 1″ x 2″ x 39″.
F. 1″ x 2″ x 19 1/2″.
G. 1″ x 2″ x 19 1/4″.
H. 1″ x 2″ x 17 7/8″.

One 30′ cedar support pole/three platforms.

Figure 21

Osprey Nest Platform

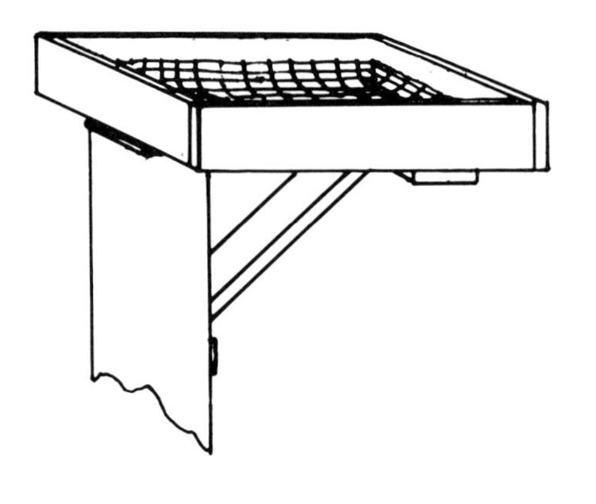

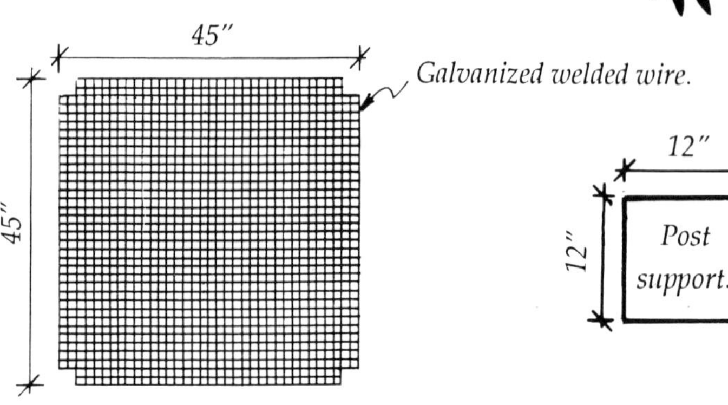

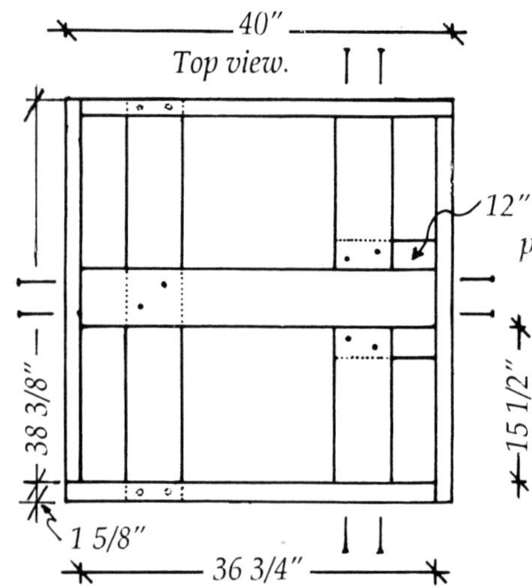

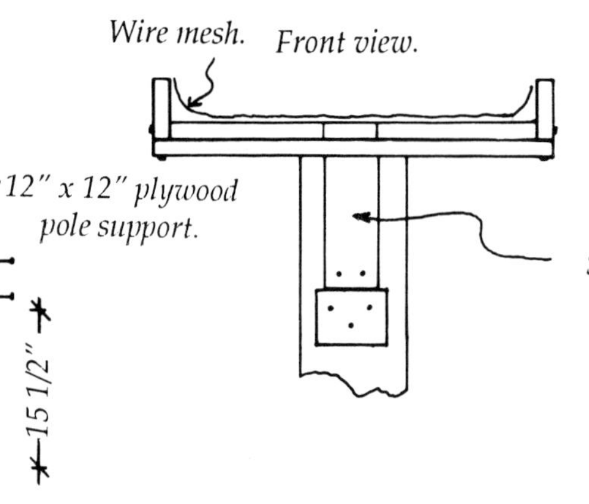

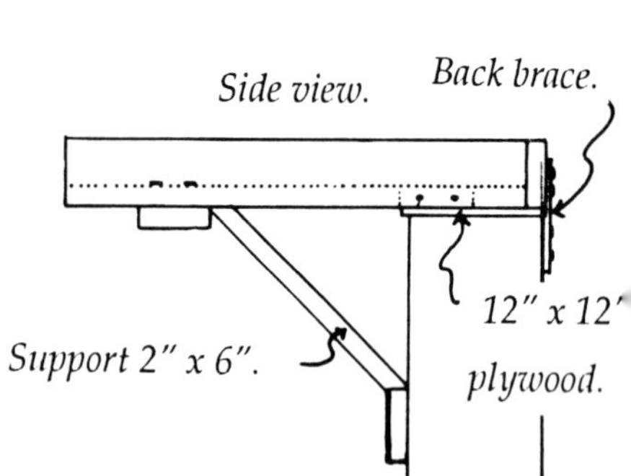

Side	Side	Base	Base
38 3/8″	38 3/8″	15 1/2″	36 3/4″

Side	Side	Base	Base
38 3/8″	38 3/8″	15 1/2″	40″

Support
Cut to desired length.

Lumber:
Two 2″ x 6″ x 12′ cedar boards.
One 2″ x 6″ x 4′ cedar board.
One 12″ x 12″ x 1/2″ exterior plywood.
One 20′ or 30′ cedar support pole.

Figure 22

Canada Goose Nest Platform
Turtle and Duck Loafing Platform

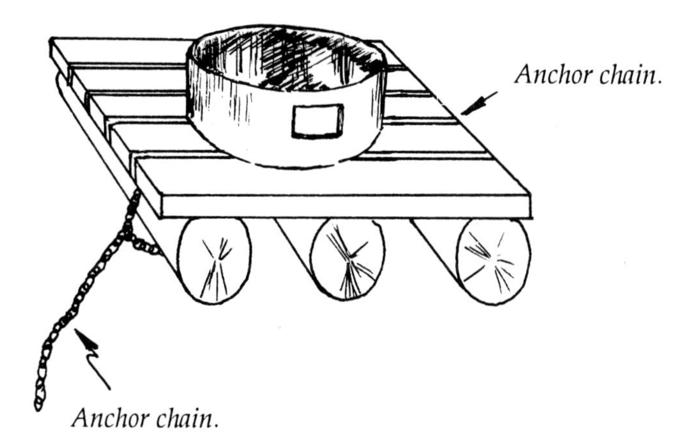

Materials:
One 8″ diameter cedar pole - 12′ long.
Four 2″ x 6″ x 8′ boards.
One 22″ diameter round metal washtub.
Do not use washtub for turtle and duck loafing platform.

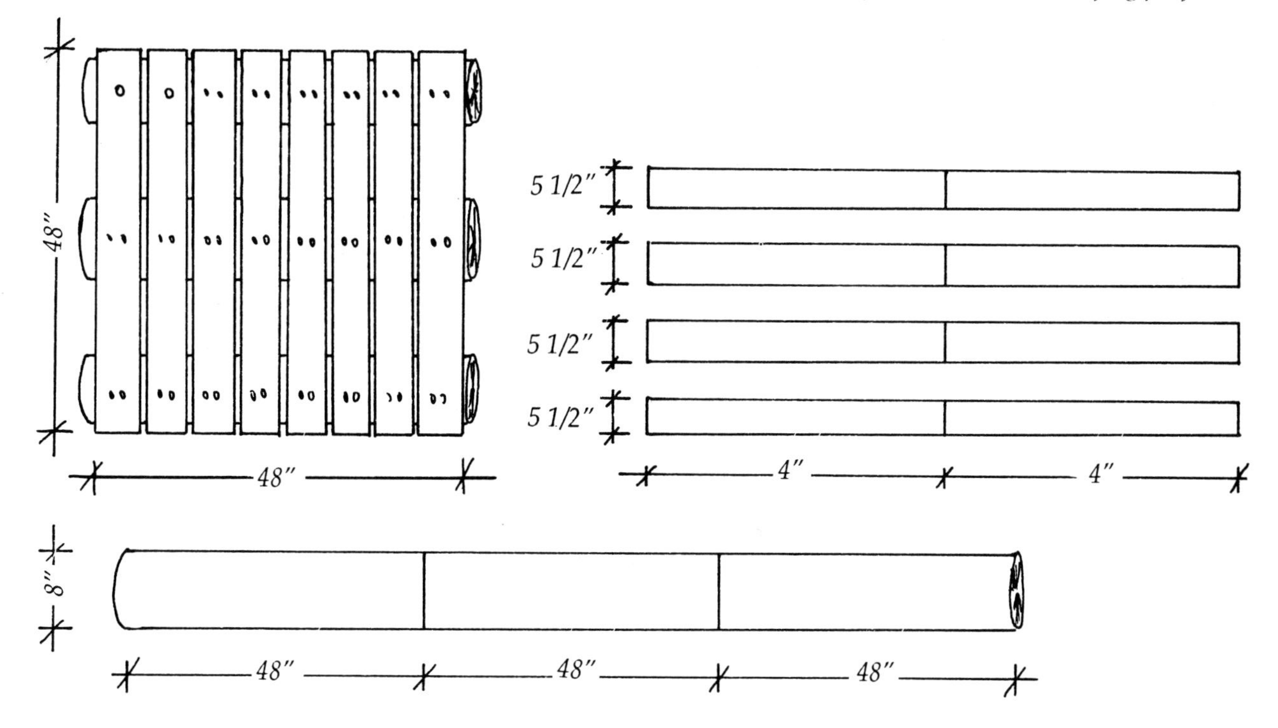

Figure 23

Forster's Tern Nest Platform

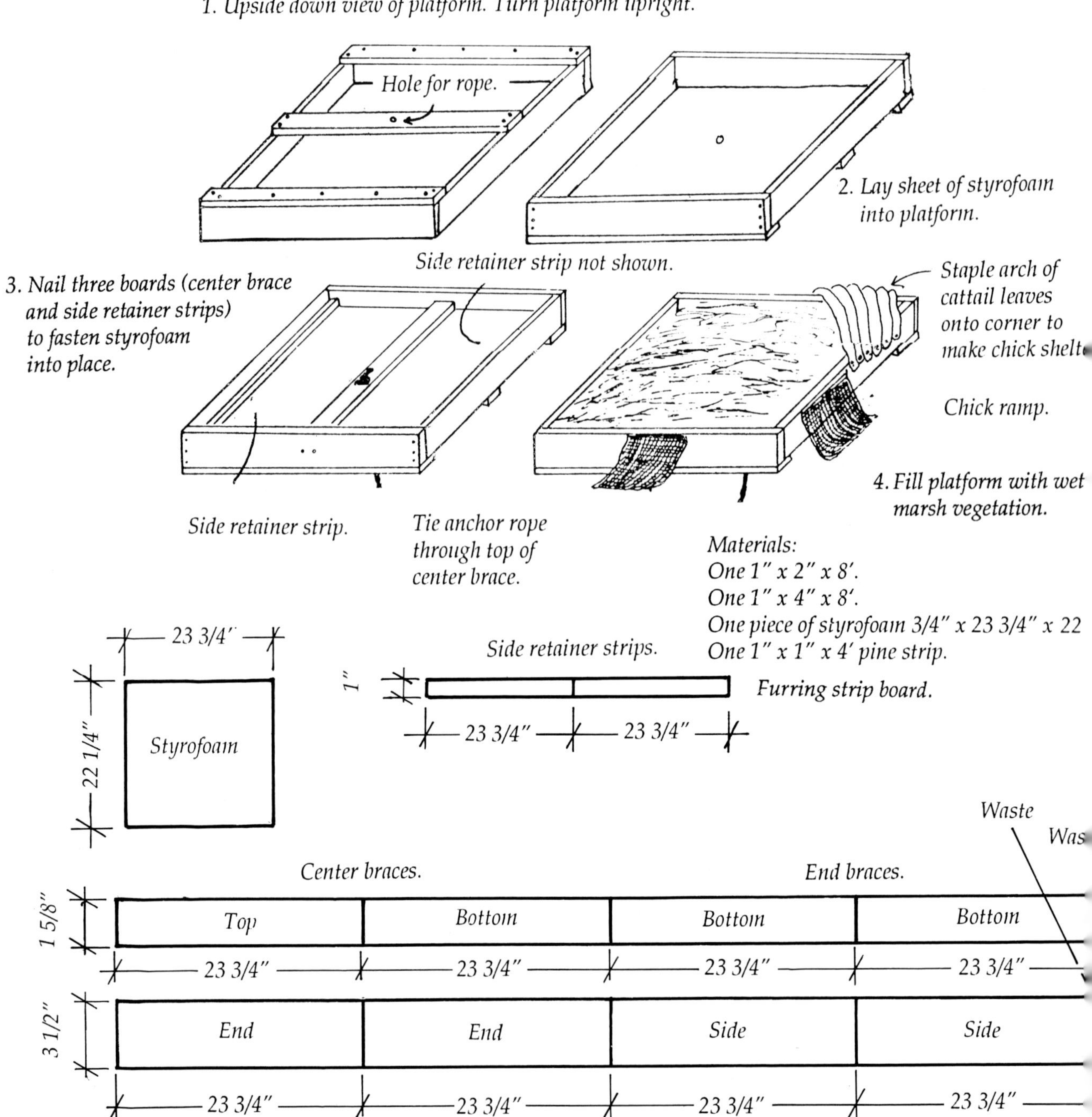

Figure 24
Cliff Swallow Nest

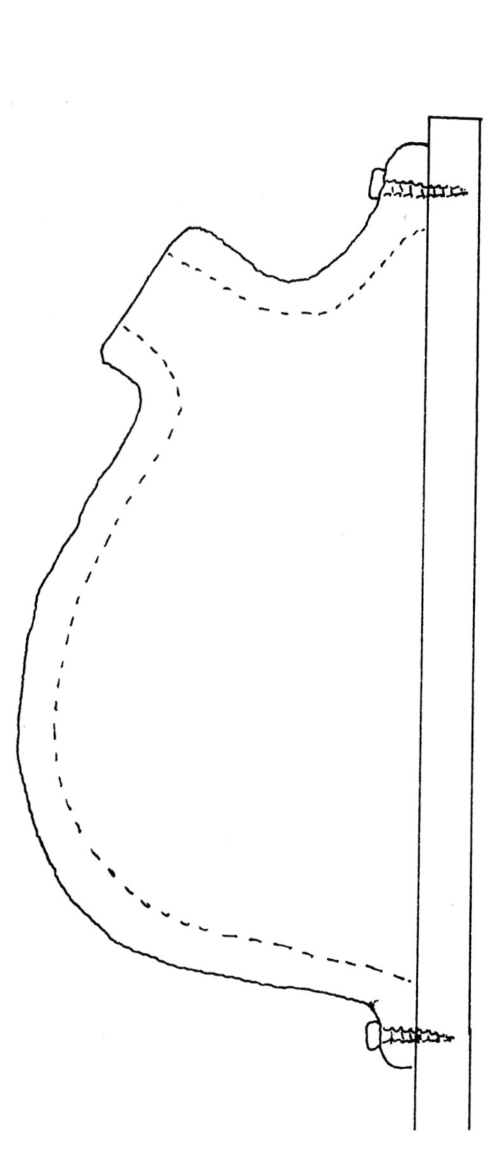

Side view of nest cross-section attached to board.

Nest sketch.

Figure 25
Mallard Nest Basket

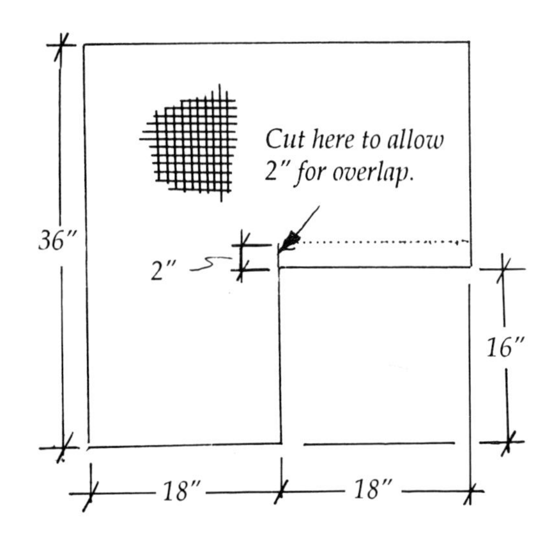

Basket pattern.

Materials:
8′ support pipe, 1 1/2″ diameter.
2′ 2″ basket pipe, 1″ diameter.
13′ 6″ steel rod, 1/4″ diameter.
3′ x 3′ hardware cloth, 1/2″ mesh.

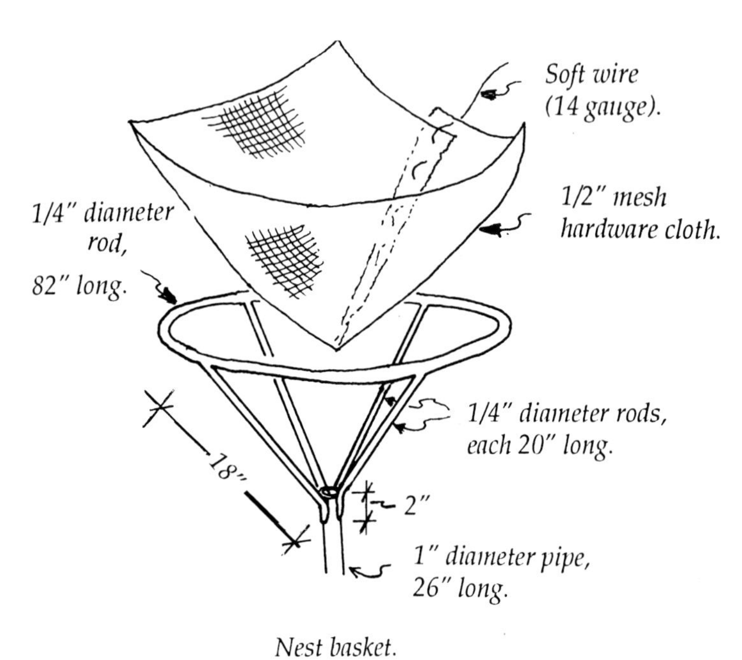

Nest basket.

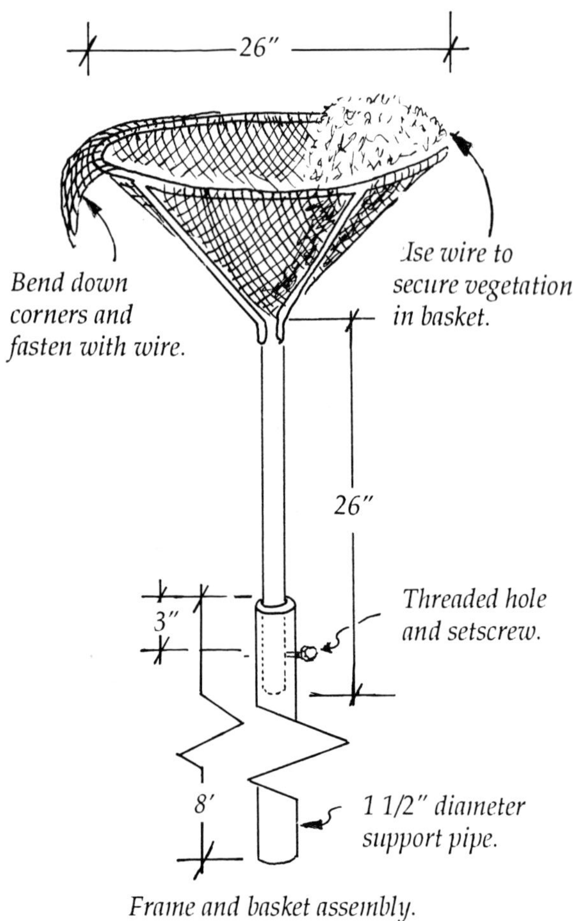

Frame and basket assembly.

Figure 26

Entrance Hole Sizes for Songbird, Woodpecker, and Squirrel Nest Boxes. Actual Size is Shown.

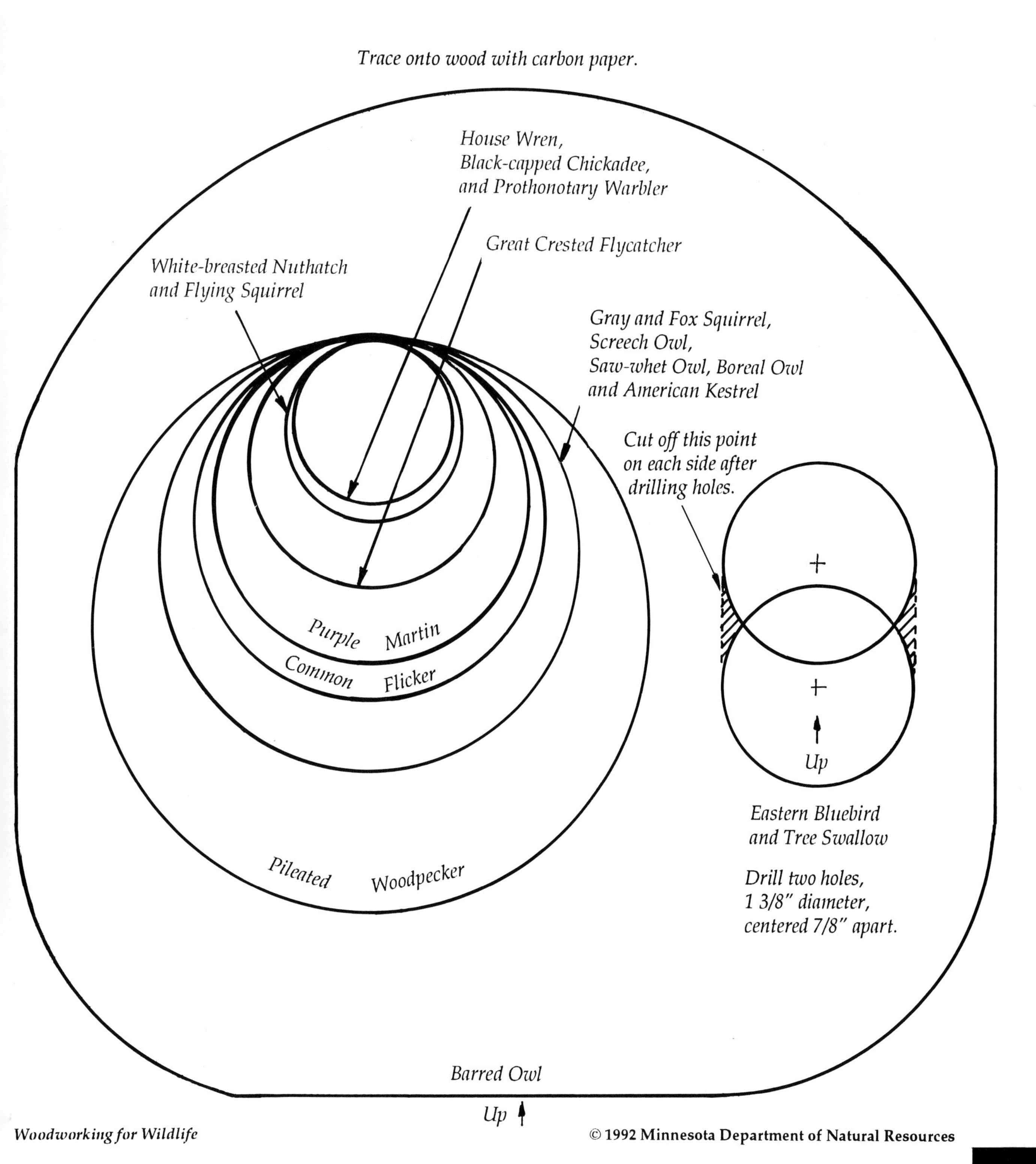

Figure 27

Entrance Hole Sizes for Duck, Merganser, and Raccoon Nest Boxes. Actual Size is Shown.

Trace onto wood with carbon paper.

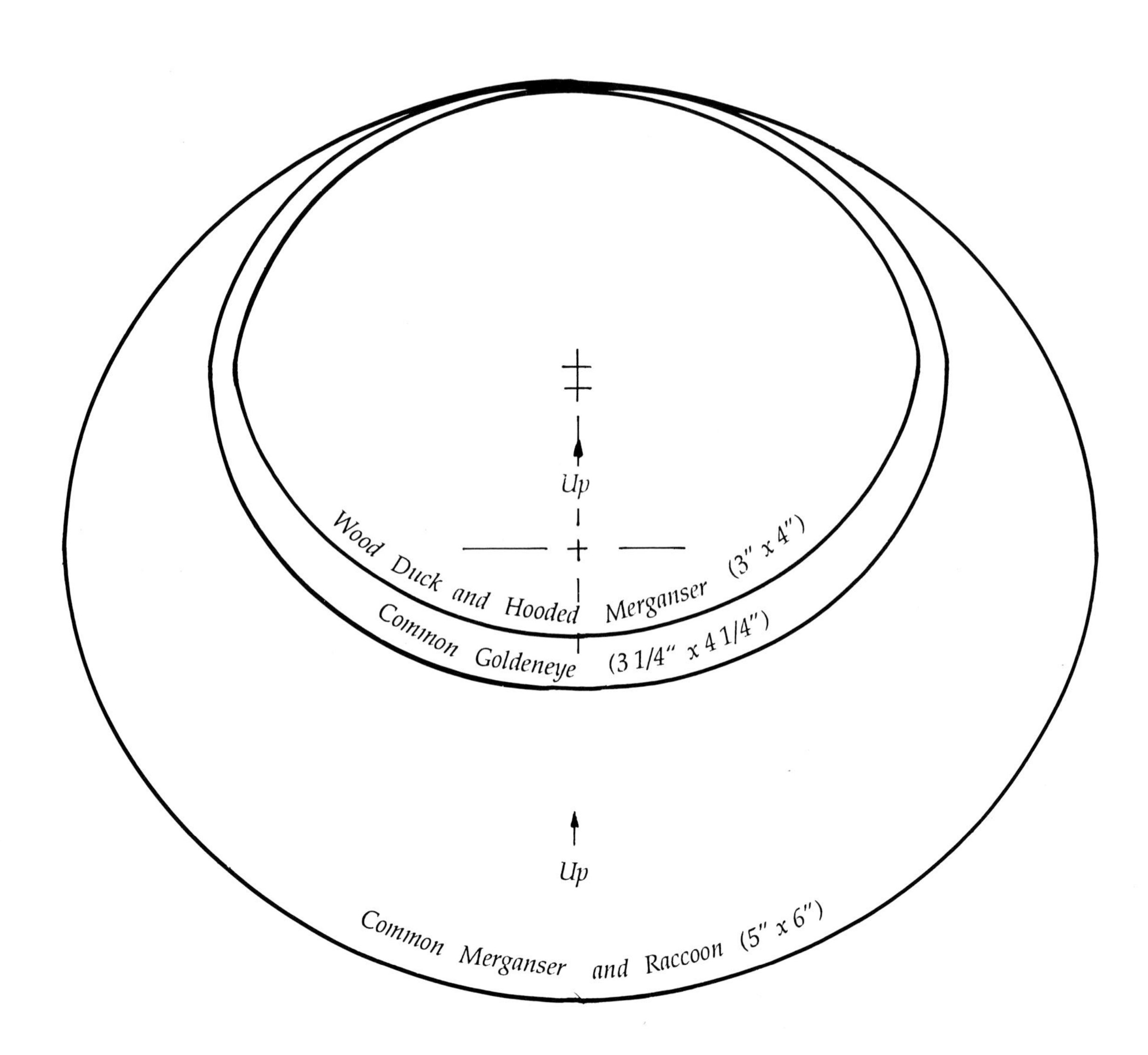

Thanks

DNR appreciates the involvement of dedicated biologists, professors, artists, photographers, and carpenters who have each contributed their expertise

Acknowledgments

This publication has been made possible by donations to the Nongame Wildlife Checkoff on Minnesota's income tax and property tax forms.

The Department of Natural Resources appreciates the involvement of these dedicated biologists, professors, artists, photographers, and carpenters who have each contributed their expertise:

Ahlgren, Dave
Andrews, Ron
Batt, Dr. Bruce
Boersma, A.J.
Bohm, Bob
Bradley, Lyle
Brooks, Bonnie
Colvin, Bruce
Craven, Dr. Scott
Cunningham, Ray
Doty, Harold
Faber, Ray
Frier, JoAnn
Galli, Joan
Hawkins, Arthur S.
Haws, Katherine
Hegdahl, Paul
Helmeke, Don
Holmes, Roger
Johnson, David (DJ)
Johnson, Ted
Jurewicz, Randy
Keran, Douglas
Loch, Steve
Longley, William H.
Mathisen, John
Mooty, Jack
Mossman, Mike
Nero, Dr. Robert
Orr-Hage, Janice
Perry, Pam
Peterson, Dick
Peterson, Ron
Scharf, John
Schladweiler, John
Schneeweis, Jim
Tuttle, Dr. Merlin
Voyer, Louis
Welton, Melinda
Wilson, Steve
Zicus, Dr. Mike

Appreciation is also extended to Dr. James H. Wilson, Dr. John Wiley, and the Missouri Department of Conservation for the original inspiration to write this book based on their publication entitled "Woodworking for Wildlife."

Nest Box Notes

Use this space to make reference notes regarding construction and maintenance of your nest boxes.